THE COLORS OF RAGE AND LOVE

To Ira
warm regards
from Bjørn
Oslo/NY   1984

THE COLORS

OF RAGE AND LOVE

The process of change in psychotherapy elucidated by the patient's own drawings

A picture book of internal events

Drawings by "Marion", the patient
Text by Marie Naevestad, the therapist

UNIVERSITETSFORLAGET
OSLO – NORWAY

© UNIVERSITETSFORLAGET 1979

ISBN 82-00-05173-0

Distribution offices:
NORWAY
Universitetsforlaget
Box 2977, Tøyen
Oslo 6

UNITED KINGDOM
Global Book Resources Ltd.
109 Great Russell Street
London WC1B 3ND

UNITED STATES and CANADA
Columbia University Press
136 South Broadway
Irvington-on-Hudson
New York 10533

PRINTED IN ENGLAND BY
THE WHITEFRIARS PRESS LTD,
LONDON AND TONBRIDGE

Contents

Acknowledgements

I gratefully acknowledge my indebtedness to "Marion" who clarified an important psychological process for me by her projection of her preconscious imagery into visible and informative symbols.

I also want to express my gratitude to my colleagues and friends at Mentalhygienisk Raadgivningskontor whose generous support, financial and otherwise, encouraged me to write this book.

I was greatly stimulated by Dr. Alberta Szalita's interest in these drawings during her visits to Norway and want to thank her for her friendly advice.

Many colleagues have guided me by giving their reactions to subsequent versions of the manuscript; though their names are not given here they are all remembered with gratitude.

I want to thank Susi Enderud for her correction of my "Scandinavian English" and the photographer Kaare Porsboell for his fine color photos and slides of Marion's drawings.

Dr. Bjoern Oestberg has been the initiator in finding a publisher for this report and I thank him for his valuable assistance.

Preface

With a few exceptions it is the therapist who tells the story of a psychotherapy. Out of the raw data given verbally by the patient, the therapist extracts the meaningfulness of the treatment process.

Here, for a change, it is the patient who tells. In this book she is called Marion. Marion, suffering from a puerperal psychosis, developed such a need for self-expression through drawing that every time by just drawing "how it felt", she reflected – quite unaware – the whole movement of a psychotherapy, from level to level of integration to a satisfying solution of her difficulties. During $2\frac{1}{2}$ years of treatment she brought her drawings to almost every session, leaving me with more than 700 pictures, all denoting her independent, creative elaboration of her struggle to face her own emotional conflicts. A relapse 8 years later, again accompanied by her drawings, will also be elaborated.

For this presentation in all 110 drawings have been selected.

Marion ended her therapy with a feeling of gratitude. She has given me her permission to use her drawings for this presentation, as she feels that psychological conflicts as well as the possibility of their solution ought to be better understood in our society.

The Use of the Adult Patient's Drawings in Psychotherapy

For the adult individual in psychotherapy, drawing may represent a creative confrontation with his or her own preconscious imagery, and the drawing then functions as an initial ordering of confused experience. A given patient may have a great ability for concretizing internal processes in pictures, and the therapist often finds this a valuable – sometimes the only possible – way of getting access to the patient's inner world. Publications have appeared presenting both the patients' pictures and the therapists' own personal way of utilizing them to help the patients identify and elaborate their conflicts (see Meares 1958, Milner 1969).

Before presenting Marion's story and drawings it may be necessary to explain how I myself in certain cases use the adult individual's often very modest ability for drawing. In my efforts to reach the mute psychotic and borderline patients I found, when a hospital psychiatrist, a way of getting access to their isolated minds. When I suggested that they should try to draw what was on their mind, this sometimes resulted in their exposition of a rich imagery, hidden behind their inability to speak. Though the patients' typical first response often was: "I cannot draw", they were reassured when I explained that the issue was not a drawing but just the outlining of a picture which was already there. Many responded at once, some only after a time of sceptical hesitation. To draw meant to communicate something without taking the risk of having to verbalize it and eventually be exposed to rejection. With an expressionless face they awaited my response, obviously ready to deny that they had communicated anything at all. The way in which I received the very first awkward drawing was of decisive significance for the patient's trust in me. When I responded with genuine interest in the drawer's conflicts, more drawings appeared. I got all sorts of "secrets" handed over to me, such as debased self-portraits in the form of despised animals, depiction of imagined, murderous crimes, early childhood memories, appalling frustrations. Those who responded, all found some way of making a picture, either using typical child-drawing, as Marion did, or else using the ordinary adult's inhibited way of naturalistic drawing. The drawings served to build up an initial contact between us, as my comments made these extremely guarded individuals feel accepted and understood. Slowly they began to talk of their own pictures which had taken them to the very heart of their suffering.

Later, in systematic long-term therapy of severely disturbed people I found that the concretization of inner imagery through projection into a picture could sometimes be of definite integrative value, assuring also that patient and therapist stood on common ground. Through drawing the patients discharged some of the excessive intensity of their affects. Typically they had been passive victims in the original traumatic situation – regularly as small children – and now they actively recreated their own version of the past events, thus slowly learning to cope with them. Better integrated, neurotic individuals will also resort to drawing from time to time, especially when some area of preverbal trauma is pressing for access to consciousness. In all cases of psychotherapy, the drawing process has been subordinated to the general technical rules of a psychoanalytically based psychotherapy, however, with flexible variations as will be observed in Marion's treatment. Verbalization and fully conscious elaboration of the drawings' symbols are always – if possible – the final aim.

Used in this frame of reference the quality of the drawings themselves is of no importance and is never commented upon; only their message is accepted to prevent giving the patient the idea that I appreciate clever drawing. Often the simplest symbols, such as spots of colour, suffice to project and communicate intense experience. Often, however, related persons will appear in the drawings. I may suggest that a certain patient should try to draw, but I never supply the patient with drawing tools, nor do I interfere with their mode of expressing themselves or give advice as regards the drawing. It is the way I comment upon the spontaneously appearing drawings, created between the sessions, that may keep the drawing process going, and the patients discover for themselves the desensitizing effect of depicting their intensely painful imagery.

It is typical for these drawings to acquire the character of secrets, of humiliating confessions, impossible to confide to anyone but the therapist and never shown to anybody else. They often represent the first signal that some area of conflict is emerging from repression, and as the released affects often are wholly un-neutralized, this process of drawing is only safe within a securely established therapeutic relationship. This will be evident from Marion's drawings. The way in which the drawing process can take hold of the patient, forcing her to report her deep inner truth in pictures, will better be demonstrated by following them here in detail.

Drawing used in this way must be thought of as an intermediate way of expressing oneself in a therapy, analogous to the child patient's drawings and play constructions. In some cases, when a more severe regression takes place, drawing may initiate a piece of child therapy within the treatment of the adult. It is then possible to communicate directly with the child-part of the patient through the pictures, while conducting a more regular psychotherapy with the adult-part. Thus the split in the patient is acknowledged, the child and the adult are both equally accepted and will unite slowly into one ego, moving towards integration and maturation. Often early splits will appear as concretely depicted figures, as the "black, angry child" and the "pale, love-starved child". The patients will spontaneously understand and accept this way of having their needs met.

As the sole value of the drawings lies in their honesty of reporting inner states, the patient must never feel obliged to please the therapist with drawings. The pictures must be met in the same neutral, factual — albeit accepting — way as other material appearing in a therapy. The drawings will accordingly, much like dreams, tend to appear or not appear in sessions, sometimes only a few drawings will appear at all, while the therapy goes on totally independent of this fact. Drawing is always of secondary and occasional significance, left to the patient's own initiative.

The pictures will afterwards simply belong to the case notes. An outside observer will rarely get any impression of the amount of affect and anxiety once projected into them, and the continuity of the developing themes will be broken time and again. Marion's great perseverance in drawing and the freshness and vitality of her drawings were quite unexpected, and a process like this, stretching over so long a period, has never occurred in any of my other patients. Marion's pictures came into being as a result of her own great ingenuity and my own interest in and way of using the patient's drawings.

I have myself never thought of this way of incorporating drawings into a therapy as anything else but a parameter of psychoanalytically oriented psychotherapy, to be welcomed and integrated when they promote the process, to be abolished when drawing becomes outgrown or when it begins to serve the resistance, or constitutes an attempt to bribe the therapist with interesting drawings. In short, their handling is not in principle different from the handling of any other material in a therapy.

Thus the presentation in this book of Marion's pictures is not primarily meant as another demonstration of the therapeutic use of drawings, which in this case was merely my own employment of a spontaneously occurring process. Nor do I regard her treatment as Art Therapy which makes use of another approach not discussed here. The drawings are published because they are very genuine and very revealing, conveying a message that has to be studied in its own right. In their own way these drawings lend support to the superstructure of psychoanalytic theories. Marion who for certain had no knowledge of psychology, simply communicated a suffering which was felt to be beyond words. The clinician finds her concrete pictorial evidence to be so rich that the material in fact can be interpreted within different frames of reference. This material accordingly also constitutes a piece of clinical research as does every deep-going therapy, and its interpretation will be discussed later in this book. After all, it is the patients themselves, through their struggle in psychotherapy, who have taught us all we know about the deeper layers of the mind.

Marie Naevestad, M.D.
Oslo, December 1977

Part I. Introduction

1. The Puerperal Depression

Marion arrived at the psychiatric ward of a general hospital at her own request in July 1962, feeling quite unable to live outside an institution for the time being. She was in a helpless, panic-stricken, despairing state of mind, imploring to be relieved of her unbearable anxiety and depression. She was a goodlooking, 23-year-old housewife, married for 2 years to a handsome craftsman, 3 years her senior. Their social conditions were satisfying.

She had born her first child, Lillian, 4 months previously. She had felt no desire for the child, but had been well during pregnancy. The labour had been uncomplicated.

When the child was there, she was unable to enjoy motherhood. During the first 3 months she had cared for the baby with a mechanical dutifulness, feeling nothing. After seeing the film "Hiroshima, my love", she had an anxiety attack, having caught a glimpse of a mutilated baby in the film. From then on her state rapidly deteriorated, with mounting anxiety which finally became impossible to control. She wept, clung to her husband in panic, and couldn't stand being left alone. She had developed such a fear of harming her child that she found it difficult to touch it at all. She felt extremely guilty about her failure as a mother and imagined herself observed by "the neighbours". Because of this threat it had lately become impossible for her to leave the house, as she then had to pass along the long row of windows from which hostile eyes were supposed to look right through her. She had lost all confidence in herself, feeling hopeless about being good enough and about ever being able to live up to the supposed rigid standards of everybody else. But what virtually crushed her and was the very essence of her disturbance, was that her mother who had been dead for 2 years, now appeared in dreams and day-time hallucinations, threatening her with eternal disaster. She "saw" her mother's stern face and "heard" her angry voice, telling her that she had no right to happiness in her life, that misery was what she deserved. Marion found no way of defending herself against this materialization of her mother, it was beyond her control. On the other hand, she complained that after the death of her mother two years ago and of her grandmother, who had died a year after her mother, she was unable to recall their looks at will. Somehow they had disappeared totally from her, they were all lost and gone, leaving her with an unbearable feeling of emptiness and futility of life.

However, in spite of this utter wretchedness, she appeared so flat and depersonalized that it was difficult for the hospital staff to feel really convinced of her despair. Between her crying spells she smilingly agreed with everyone. Her manners were extremely compliant, active manifestations of aggression were totally absent, and she was unable to assert herself in the company of her fellow patients. As the ward was organized as a therapeutic community, with much involvement between staff and patients, these character traits were easily recognizable. She consequently earned the diagnosis of a hysterical puerperal depression. Her symptoms were of psychotic dimensions, but she was never found to be clinically psychotic.

2. The Story

Marion's father, a sailor, had died before she was born. His family lived far away, and no contact was maintained with his people. Her mother never talked of him. After his death she had returned to her own parents in town, pregnant with her first child. Here Marion was born and had her home during all her childhood.

The grandfather was a rather distant person to Marion and died when she was a child. The grandmother was a housewife, caring for her family in a small, old house of their own on the outskirts of the town, where some of her mother's sisters and brothers were still living. None of the men in her family ever became a father figure for Marion, but she was closely attached to a male cousin, who was a good, big brother and play-mate for her. The whole setting was one of a typical working class family of rather proud and independent people.

In Marion's first description of her childhood, her mother had lived with her in the old house till Marion was nine. She had been told that her mother had breastfed her, staying at home for some time before resuming her work. This was the happy time when she "had her mother". Marion said that she had loved and admired her mother, and described her as a beautiful, vigorous and temperamental woman, who had supported herself and her child as a saleswoman. However, Marion could also tell that her mother had little time left for her child. After a long, laborious day she often dressed up and went out with her friends to enjoy herself, much to Marion's dismay. During the summer holidays Marion regularly was sent to camp instead of being allowed to stay with her mother. She hated the camp, and once ran away and went home, preferring the streets of the town to the country if she only could be with her mother.

The grandmother, to whom Marion was deeply attached, was a stable and loving support all through her childhood. "Grandmother had a great understanding of children", Marion told me. Grandmother never interfered with Marion's play and her behavior of natural self-expression, and was quite relaxed when Marion soiled herself and used the curse-words of her playmates in the street. Her mother was different. She punished her child severely when she didn't behave according to her own standards. As Marion later could put it: "Grandmother loved me as I was, in my own right. Mother always urged me to be otherwise, somebody else than myself. She wanted me to be obedient and nice, clean and well-dressed, grandmother didn't care about all that. Grandmother was the only one who could stand up against my mother's anger. She always protected me".

Because of her mother's violent temper, Marion was intimidated by her and was never able to express the resentment she felt towards her. But there was also much of a rich and happy togetherness, the conflicts were to some extent open.

Marion was able to defy her mother, then taking refuge with her grandmother.

When Marion was nine, her mother re-married and left the common household. She settled in the same town, and Marion visited her regularly. The half-sister Ellen was born. Without any explanation Marion was left behind with her grandparents.

Marion described this event as a paralysing shock. "Mother left me". "I lost my mother". She dated the onset of her difficulties to this overwhelming trauma, which was experienced as the loss of her mother's love. In her therapy it by and by became evident that she had linked this loss to her own disobedience and defiance. It was conceived of as the most dreadful punishment for her hidden anger; she didn't deserve to be loved. Only much later in her therapy did Marion become fully aware of the amount of repressed rage she had felt towards her mother from her earliest childhood. She remembered later that her mother had not always lived permanently with her in the old house before her marriage. From time to time she had left the crowded household and found herself some other place to live where Marion visited her. During the first period of her therapy, however, the loss of the love relation to her mother overshadowed everything else.

After the shock of her mother's marriage Marion had suppressed all expression of negative feelings, afraid to lose what was left her of approval and love. She became outwardly submissive and obedient, and the genuine emotional contact with her mother was lost. The desperate yearning for a reunion with her, the hate for being abandoned, and the murderous wishes for Ellen to disappear again, could nowhere find expression. It was impossible even to tell her grandmother of such evil. Inside herself she locked up an image of a cruel, deceitful and rejecting mother, while the good mother was now seen as belonging entirely to Ellen. In her jealousy she was exposed to the torments of Tantalus by every visit. This deterioration in her relationship with her mother greatly influenced her further maturation. She didn't outgrow and overcome her childish demandingness and dependence upon her mother through a natural and open interrelation with her; she remained with her hate and her angry urge to recover her mother. As her feelings were all bottled up, she was doomed from now on to carry within her the burden of these intensely negative feelings, which may be described as an internalized, bad mother.

Her stepfather was a difficult man, who had no relationship to offer her. Her mother divorced him after some years of marriage, and he later went abroad and remarried.

After nine years of school, Marion started to work as a shop girl. She developed no special interests. At the age of 17 she began to go steady with her later husband, who remembered her from that time as a gay and attractive girl.

But then her mother, now divorced, asked the 17-year-old Marion to come and live with her and Ellen, and this caused a revival of the earlier conflicts. Marion left her grandmother, hoping to be reconciled with her mother, only to discover that she was unable to control her own unkindness towards both her mother and her half-sister. She stayed for a year, feeling all the time unhappy and guilty, stuffing herself with food as a consolation. She left impulsively after a quarrel with her mother, hoping until the last minute that her mother would stop her at the door, and that they at last would be able to talk things through. But nothing happened, and Marion settled down with her grandmother again, now tortured with guilt-feeling towards both of them, not knowing where she belonged. In her despair she now decided to make herself independent of her attachment to her mother. She chose the irrational solution of going on a diet and lost her appetite and joy in food for years. Her menstruation became irregular, disappearing for months. She also developed a compulsive perfectionism which she hadn't known in herself before. She had always been leaning upon the relaxed standards of her grandmother; from now on, however, she became aware of how greatly she feared the criticism of others. The mother whom she intended leaving thus seemed to make herself felt from within. At this time the 18-year-old Marion felt so miserable that she on her own consulted a psychiatrist, whose tablets and friendly words proved to be of no help to her. One here sees the symptoms of an incipient anorexia nervosa, that pathetic psychic illness in which the attempt to control interpersonal difficulties is replaced by the compulsive rejection of food. The condition, however, never developed beyond this stage.

Her mother developed cancer and died in 1960 when Marion was 21. This irretrievable loss was met with frozen, tearless despair. When her grandmother died the next year, Marion was just as unable to mourn. She felt she had no right to miss her grandmother, as he had felt quite cold when her mother had died. From now on she felt depressed and rootless and lost her joy in sex. Her mother caused her anxiety by frequently appearing in her dreams. She married her friend shortly afterwards, needing someone to hold on to. An element of clinging cast its shadow on this relationship, she felt it later not to have been a truly free choice. Her mother had advised her to marry him, and when Marion later revolted against her own submissiveness, the marriage for a long time was conceived of as mainly an act of compliance with her mother. Besides, her mother-in-law exposed Marion to the most difficult aspect of her relationship with her mother: the feeling of not being good enough. Marion was extremely vulnerable to the critical attitude of her mother-in-law, and had reacted with servility and unhappiness, hoping in vain that some day she would be loved and accepted.

In contrast, she was profoundly fond of her father-in-law. With him she again felt the trust and support that had been so fundamental in her relationship with her grandmother. However, this was her story seen in retrospect, when all the pieces of the picture puzzle had fallen into place. It was not at all that clear when Marion started her treatment.

3. The Psychiatric Treatment

The treatment plan of the psychiatric ward was rather a good one for an approach on this level of the therapeutic endeavor. The ward was open, with a milieu program of daily groups and activities, offering the patients much opportunity for self-expression and for forming new relationships. The contact with her home was insured by frequent leaves. Her child was hospitalized together with her, and the nurses tried to help her to gain confidence in herself as a mother.

Her special contact was a young, male doctor who took much interest in her. She had regular individual sessions with him, as well as joint sessions with her husband in marriage therapy.

Her doctor thus tried to integrate her again with her family life and to reach her accessible conflicts and have them worked through. He noticed that when he touched upon her conspicuous lack of aggression, her depression at once deepened to an alarming degree. He had to give it up and try to calm down the deeper disturbances by drugs. In a period of suicidal preoccupation she had 4 ECTs (electro-shock-treatments).

Some slight improvement was every time followed by a relapse and a reappearance of each of her symptoms. The core of her disturbance was not accessible. She was compulsively preoccupied with her dead mother, a helpless victim to her mother's cruel condemnation, and she was full of remorse and guilt because their conflicts had not been solved in time. Nor was there any improvement in her relation to her child.

Her doctor, having faith in her resources, then tried to secure a long-term treatment for her by a psychiatrist in private practise. She returned from her first session with him, tearful and upset, and refused to go back to him.

The first time she stayed at the hospital for 6 months (July 1962–March 1963). After leaving she remained in contact with her hospital doctor as an outpatient. She had to be rehospitalized for 4 weeks during the summer of 1963 (August–September), as much weighed down by her persecutory and depressive anxieties as before. Her doctor now tried actively to divert her from her lamentations of past unhappiness, advising her to live HERE AND NOW and to attend to her real life with her husband and child.

When she was hospitalized for the third time in October 1963, he gave her up. It was evident that the treatment had to be continued on a different level of therapy. He asked me to try a psycho-analytically oriented psychotherapy, for which he himself was not trained.

4. Psychoanalytically Based Psychotherapy

I worked at the hospital and already knew Marion from the milieu therapy. Like her doctor, I also had faith in her resources. In spite of her actual misery, one sensed a robust vitality beneath, and I hoped to find a way of releasing her from the spell cast by her dead mother. Marion herself was reluctant and frightened at the prospect of a therapy she neither had asked for, nor wanted and, in addition, she was

unhappy at being deserted by her doctor of whom she was very fond. However, she had no choice. She had been told that "deep psychotherapy" could be her only way out of a state of chronic illness, and she knew that her next stay would probably be in the mental hospital. Again she stayed for 6 months (October 1963–March 1964). This time her child was left behind with her mother-in-law.

During this third hospital stay we worked through the first layer of her intensely negative feelings towards her mother, stepfather, and half-sister Ellen, and the guilt-feelings accompanying these emotions. When she became more aware of her own rage towards her mother, the result was that the reflection of this hate, the mother inside herself who was felt to hate Marion, lost a little of its harshness. Her jealousy of Ellen had extended to everybody else, in fact all over her existence. She believed everybody else to be happy, enjoying their warm relationships with each other, being filled with rich happiness. Only she herself was left out, empty and lonely, without a meaningful relationship to anyone. Her husband and child had each other, while she lived in the darkness, without hope. Her husband also had his parents, without including her. Ellen, who after the death of their mother lived with relatives in the country, had at that time, 16 years old, already born a child but not yet married her boyfriend. She had been helped by her family to care for the child herself. Marion at this time had little contact with her. Ellen was now conceived of as still "having" the good mother inside herself, while Marion had lost her mother inwardly. Ellen was the rich and lucky one, who also "had" her child and was a happy mother. This meant to Marion that there existed a delightful, close, warm one-ness, a bodily, sensuous contact between Ellen and her mother, still preserved in the interior of Ellen. Because of this, Ellen was able to have just the same sort of relation to her child. Marion was desperate in her hunger for this sort of bodily sensuous closeness which, for reasons she couldn't understand, was barred to her. In January 1964 Ellen once visited the town, bringing a kitten with her. The supposed cozy nuzzling between cat and sister made Marion wild with despair in her pining for just this sort of affectionate cuddling. The very intensity of this hunger seemed to point to a fatal break in Marion's contact with her mother at some early age, when this bodily contact had been the very essence of her mother's presence. Ellen who once joined us in a session, was a shy and unassuming girl. It was striking to see how Marion, who had all sorts of "good things" in her life: a handsome husband with a good income, a nice apartment, a child, a car, felt herself miserably poor and empty in comparison with Ellen, who owned nothing but was supposed to possess the good mother within herself.

Marion discovered that she transferred her hatred of Ellen to her own child. When she tried to mother it, it invariably "changed into Ellen". Marion's rage and envy intervened and blocked all warmth and possibilities of close contact. She was then afraid of harming Lillian. At other times, her own yearning for a mother so overwhelmed her when she was to care for her child, that she began to cry and had to give it up, unable to bear the intensity of her emotions. Even with a growing insight into these facts, she was quite unable emotionally to discriminate between past and actual, between inner and outer reality.

Her resentment of her mother-in-law also came to the fore, since the latter was unable to be a new, good mother to Marion. And toward the end of this hospital stay, her anger reached her husband. She thought of her marriage as a dull prison into which she had been manipulated by her mother. She had yielded because of her own apathy and inertia after her mother's death. Now she was condemned to eternal slavery for husband and child, without feeling any joy and meaningfulness on her own behalf. Here, at least, a confrontation with reality was possible. Her husband was invited for a sequence of marriage therapy. Her protest against him was seen to be the first sign of a revolt against her own extreme submissiveness, at first projected onto her husband of whose tyranny and domination she now complained. The spouses talked their conflicts through. It became evident that by her own passivity and inability to decide anything, she had driven him to take action. She had been afraid of asserting herself, as this unconsciously had for her the implied meaning of being abandoned and turned down. Her conviction that self-expression was bad and would lead to a loss of love had thus been generalized to the extent of paralyzing her capacity to express her feelings directly, causing resentment to accumulate beneath.

After this marriage therapy, the relation between the partners improved. As Marion had been able to express herself relatively freely during this treatment period, she developed as a result some new self-reliance. For the first time she started to play with colored crayons in the workshop of the hospital, experiencing during this play a state of mind that reminded her of her happy days as a child. When she left the hospital in March 1964 she was quite optimistic. She continued the therapy with me as an out-patient once a week.

Some thinning out of her symptoms had been the result of our work. No deeper change had occurred, however. In November 1964 she was again intensely depressed. I now suggested that she should try to draw, remembering the flash of joy she had felt when drawing during the last weeks of her hospital stay. I hoped for more active self-expression. She still was essentially compliant and self-effacing.

5. Marion's Drawings

She responded at once and brought her pictures to the sessions, mainly of flowers and birds, occasionally of some little girl and a mother figure. They were plain children's drawings but playfully and spontaneously drawn, and they stood in a curious contrast to her flat, depersonalized way of talking. It was all rather disorganized, her drawings were scattered around the paper in a rather haphazard fashion, and I could detect no immediate connection between these drawings and her own, conflict-ridden self.

I received them with respect and interest as something created by her, dated them, and put them in my drawer. During November and December 1964 I got 50 of them, but none of them are presented here. She didn't associate to them, in fact she had very little to say about them. But to her they were meaningful; she became clearly absorbed in drawing from the very first time she tried it. This first period of carefree play probably prepared the ground for her later ability to project her own world of experience into the drawings.

In January 1965 she felt much improved. For the first time since the birth of Lillian she took a part-time job as a shop assistant, had Lillian placed in a kindergarten, and proposed to see me only once in a fortnight. She stopped drawing, but in February 1965 she spontaneously took it up again, from then on during the next $2\frac{1}{2}$ years – with the aid of her own drawings – traveling a road that was to take her to the very core of her disturbance.

6. The Structure of Marion's Drawings

This presentation is a retrospective study of her drawings. My reflections, accompanying her pictures, are afterthoughts of today. At the time of their occurrence I neither had the time nor the need to scrutinize them. They were integrated in the ongoing therapy, much like the images of a dream, often incompletely understood. Even though her drawings – her homework between the sessions – served her own liberation to an inestimable degree, their presentation never occupied much time of the session itself, but fitted naturally into the overall context of our verbal interaction. In fact, they thrived at being a little out of focus, and her feeling that this was her own, independent, creative contribution to the therapy was never lost. Thus the drawings kept their innocence and spontaneity during all this time. They were never shown to anybody else but her therapist.

These drawings are exceptional in more than one way. For the first, the compelling urge to draw didn't subside, even in periods of great crisis. She *had* to express what was stirring in her, feeling drawing to be her only way of self-realization at that time, even continuing it on her own during the long summer holiday. Secondly, her pictures reflect the same level of psychic depth all through this treatment period of 2½ years. One theme grows logically out of the other, giving the whole series a unique coherence and wholeness. One may postulate that the sheet of paper symbolizes her area of integration and differentiation, giving us her own picture of her inner world with its drama of subtle change and growth, as well as of sudden transformations in the structure of her drawings.

In order to understand more of the structure of this way of drawing one has to turn to genuine child drawing. When one consults an expert in this field, V. Lowenfeld (1959), it becomes evident that Marion's level of expression approximates his description of the Schematic Stages of the child between 7 and 9 years of age. The peculiarities of her pictures, the repetitions, the consistency of her color and form symbols as well as her way of expressing herself through the movements and the relative size given to each of her figures – all these are typical features of child drawing at this stage of development. Repetitions do not here imply rigidity or lack of spontaneity; they are natural and necessary for mastery and self-assurance. For Marion they meant a gradual mastering of her conflicts through confronting them in her own drawings, thereby slowly desensitizing her against their agonizing pain that at first had caused her to flee in panic.

Also, the use of a definite concept for a long time is typical of this age. The child struggles to form his personal scheme of the human figure, of objects and of relationships. Drawing is at this level an unaware creative expression of emotional experience, and the child can project only what is real and true to himself. A change of his scheme is only possible when some impression of sufficient intensity interferes with the old pattern and changes it according to the new experience. When Marion has worked out her concept of an actual inner constellation which is felt to be true, it remains unaltered for a long time but for variations within the main structure, and it is definitely established through repetitions till she is ready for a new concept. Due to these repetitions, all her themes, including the few that occurred just once, are represented in this book.

Her human scheme initially consists of a triangle of geometrical lines, with roughly drawn symbols for head, arms, and legs and corresponds to the typical child drawing of this age. This scheme is only altered toward the end of the therapy when the mature female body with breasts and hips appears. Also a rigid adherence to the same color for the same objects is typical of the child. The choice of color is highly subjective, determined by the child's experience at the time when he discovered that certain objects have a definite color. The color scheme remains unaltered for a long time, till again some experience is important enough to change it. Marion's use of her own subjective color scheme is of intense emotional significance to herself and remains unaltered through the whole period of the first therapy between February 1965 and October 1967.

According to Lowenfeld, the child uses typical variations within the chosen schemes to express situations and experience in a flexible and vivid way. These are of three principal types:

1. Human figures or parts of their bodies may be exaggerated in size, or some parts may be neglected or omitted, and accordingly drawn small or not at all. It is not difficult to find illustrations of this in Marion's drawings. Her half-sister, when taken out of her confinement, overwhelms Marion and turns into a huge being, while Marion's supporting world shrinks (drawing of 13 August 1965). She omits her own eyes when she tries to persuade herself that she is looking on the newborn sister in a friendly way (drawing of 15 November 1965). Marion grows bigger with ever longer arms when she angrily proceeds to retrieve her mother (drawing of 15 November 1965).

2. Another deviation is that of a change of form when some part of the body acquires a special emotional significance. Marion is more liable to use size relationships to express herself, but we see the latter variant when, for example, the subhuman figure breaks through its fence, acquiring a black hand in its search for human contact. In one picture even five naturalistically drawn human fingers (drawing of 11 September 1965) are seen. The therapist is portrayed as a witch with a long nose and a broom when Marion's negative feelings are in ascendance.

3. The third variant uses the characterization of relationships between figures to express meaning. Marion uses a wide variation of relationships, such as clinging, fight, safety on the lap, etc. In fact, these depicted relationships are the very essence of her non-verbal communication and highly informative to the observer who is able to witness their changing quality.

Another sign that Marion approximates to this level of maturity is the occurrence in her drawings of "folding over". This means that a part of the drawing, which from the point of view of the drawer could not be visible, is folded over in order to become visible. This happens when Marion draws her mother's house. The wall with the window of mother's bedroom is on the opposite side of the house, but this window is of such emotional significance that the wall is folded over, and the window appears in the drawing (drawing of 9 April 1965).

Lowenfeld analyses the origin of these deviations in child drawing. For the first there is the subjective feeling of one's own self, the self-image, which becomes projected into the drawing. Marion grows or is reduced in size, she occupies the center of the drawing or is pushed towards the edge of the paper. Also the muscular tensions, the stirring of motor impulses of which the drawer isn't yet aware, causes her to put motion into an arm or into the whole drawn figure. The re-experience of the picture makes the drawer feel this movement in her own body. Nothing frightens Marion more than these impulses which press for release, and which she at first often perceives in her own drawings.

Secondly, there is the subjective judgement of value; what is positively evaluated is emphasized in some way. Emotional value is to a great extent expressed by Marion through her good colors, orange and yellow.

And lastly the emotional significance, whether any situation is good or bad, greatly influences the scheme.

Be it the real child of nine or the child in Marion who creates pictures of such a structure, it becomes rather evident that drawing at this level of maturity is controlled by emotional reality beyond the drawer's deliberate intentions. We know that a major trauma occurred when she was nine, and we may wonder whether her emotional development was arrested to such an extent that, when the chance came for a liberation, she had to tell it all in a language appropriate to a child of nine.

The evidence brought forward here justifies us in paying attention to what she has revealed through her drawings. They represent the structures and processes of the mind to the same extent as do the dreams, the transference reactions and the associations on which the therapist builds her conclusions. I propose that we trust her and go on to observe the material at hand.

Part II
Presentation of the Drawings

7. Dissociation. 21 Drawings

6 February 1965

In January 1965 we had both hoped for a lasting stabilization. She now seemed to have gained sufficient strength through the treatment to be able to manage without my aid. We had no contract beyond this; she had no conscious wish to penetrate deeper into her disturbance. She would be one of the many psychiatric patients in whom only a therapeutic plan minimum had been realized.

What impulse made her take to drawing again? Had the way I received her first unassuming drawings unconsciously convinced her of my willingness to understand metaphorical communication? This time the initiative was wholly her own; again she brought her plants and birds to the sessions. However, her pictures had now changed. They were of a far greater coherence and certainty, organized in a far more definite way of self-representation in the centre of the paper. They were forceful and expressive, but what they communicated was at that time not easy to understand. They belonged to a level of their own, obviously engaging her intensely. I again thought of them as a means of self-expression now being opened up to her, and I shared her interest in them. She hadn't much to say about them, and I let them be too, dating them, asking how she felt about them, and then putting them away in my drawer.

This is one of her first plants in this new series of drawings. She was drawing with a surprising ease. The freedom, rhythm, and balance of her drawings revealed a creative potential which had been impossible to detect through merely her verbal communication. They were drawn without the slightest ambition; there was never a trace of erasure or correction in any one of the 700 drawings that were to follow upon these first ones. She had chosen colored crayon for her pictures and never changed her drawing implements during the next $2\frac{1}{2}$ years. Some very provoking themes, however, had always to be tried out in pencil first, before she dared to invest color in them.

12 February 1965

During the sessions we are sitting face to face, talking to each other. It is up to Marion herself to choose the moment of presenting her drawings, her homework between the sessions. Here is another of her typical early drawings, this time of a bird. Spontaneously she began to associate to her pictures, telling me how painful they were to make. She had to be alone and concentrate intensely to grasp her visual imagery and concretize it in a drawing. It all had to do with her own misery and her relation to her mother. She lost her distance to pain during the act of drawing and often became overwhelmed and had to cry. "This violet and dark green reminds me of mother – of the suffering I connect with her ..."

"this is what is hanging over me all the time, the depression, the futility of it all ... It is my fear of everybody else, of the neighbors ..."

From now on violet and dark green will represent the all-bad aspects of her mother in every drawing. Her color scheme is establishing itself. Also, the process of projecting her personal experience into the drawings is manifesting itself. It is the total area of her symptoms, her persecutory anxieties, her depression and hopelessness which are condensed in these drawings, all of them embodying her mother's bad colors. The drawings slowly began to change and vitalize the therapy. The clinical improvement seemed to be just a prerequisite for these first, daring steps into the unknown. On the basis of her own, creative work access was gained to a deeper psychic level, and she began to talk in a more personal way, her language now becoming rooted in her own emotional experience. Somehow her talking till now had seemed to be just a language of compliance.

The bird has something in its beak, a little fish-like object, a sort of duplication of itself. Could it be Marion? Though not mentioned by Marion or at that time perceived by myself, I should now, in the light of the later development, suggest that this little being may represent Marion in a state of symbiotic undifferentiation from her mother.

For four weeks to come a central, non-human figure will be seen, taking on fantastic variations of shape, all of them sinister, threatening, monster-like and associated with her mother.

24

13 February 1965

I began to record her associations to the drawings. In this presentation I shall deliberately leave out most of the process evolving from our verbal interaction; it was a regular psychotherapy, slowly connecting her symptoms with her personal experience and consistently preventing her flight from her conflicts. Her attitude to me was at this time mildly positive, interrupted by angry demands for a less painful help or by accusations of not helping her at all: "You are always taking me back to the painful issues . . . I want to forget about it all . . ." Her desperate claims for some new drugs or more ECTs recurred time and again. Some medicine had in fact been necessary all the time to alleviate the intensity of her anxiety and depression and to keep this therapy going at all.

On a deeper level, however, she must have known that this confrontation with internal reality was necessary, because she on her own continued drawing. As I found myself involved in a difficult verbal therapy, I hadn't yet discovered how accurately these drawings were to reflect the process of inner change. I welcomed them, but was far from realizing the full significance of her intuitive communication. Thus when – as here – a new entity appeared in the drawing, an orange worm creeping along the edge of the paper, my comments are of today. Of this worm she herself said: ". . . these orange and light green belong to myself . . . they are *my* colors. I'm fond of them . . ."

Orange is added to her color scheme and will have the fixed, unalterable meaning of goodness in all later drawings. It will differentiate itself as love, as warmth, as a beginning core of selfhood, as resources – in short we may conceive of it as the symbol of libido. A tiny emotional self-representation has evidently come into existence, beside the threatening, central form – the symbol of her symptoms and her mother. To the right another sort of bird is seen, in yellow. Such birds will later appear from time to time and then be identified by Marion as the "birds of flight", representing her wish to flee from what happens in the drawing. To come into existence – even as a creeping worm – seems to imply some danger. I didn't realize this, and Marion was just as unaware of it.

I should have taken more notice of this bird of flight. There was another signal too that something was stirring in her. She asked to see me once a week, instead of once a fortnight, as she herself had proposed in early January.

20 February 1965A

Here again this small, orange something appears, in between many drawings where it doesn't appear at all. The monster has grown in size, filling out the paper almost entirely, pushing the orange "me" into the corner, where it seems to struggle to maintain itself at all. Another warning signal escaped me which I later learnt to be attentive to: when something "dangerous" in her drawing grew in size, there would be a risk that her mounting anxiety would become unmanageable.

In fact, Marion at this time struggles to maintain herself in real life. She works in the shop but experiences a growing alarm within her for which she has no explanation. She has increasing difficulties in leaving her home.

It may be time to review Marion's inner state at this stage of her therapy. She had suffered a partial psychosis in 1962 after the birth of Lillian, comprising mainly the disturbed relationship to her dead mother and to her child, true to a typical puerperal depression. The therapy till now had strengthened her by making her conscious of and working through much of her rage, guilt and generalized jealousy and had helped her to gain some new self-confidence. She was able to push aside much of her anxieties and depression and go on with her daily life. However, the core of her disturbance had not been touched. She was still unable to meet her child's need for emotional warmth and closeness, and there was no investment in sexual intimacy with her husband. In fact, her actual libidinal relationships were depleted of vitality and love. Seen in retrospect, her drawings caused a surge in the whole area of disturbance. They here begin to reveal a certain structure. An attempt to separate herself from a distorted, primitive mother image seems to take place. Something in her evidently had remained un-differentiated, while another part of her had been able to grow up.

Let us assume that the orange "me" is the birth or rebirth of a libidinal core of selfhood, perhaps the first appearance of the "true self" in Winnicott's sense. (Winnicott 1975 [1950].)

20 February 1965B

By and by the good orange "me" has come to stay, from now on it is represented in every drawing. Here, in the shadow of the overwhelming bird, it is a little more differentiated and has acquired a head and two arms, still not distinctly drawn. The struggle to be has begun. This is a process deep down in her, still unconscious, only betrayed by her drawings. Here she seems to stretch out her arms toward a rather unapproachable object. There isn't much communication in this relationship. Does Marion unknowingly recreate an experience from her earliest childhood – her own appeal to an unavailable mother? At least, such a constellation is coming to the fore in her drawings.

At the same time something else happens which will also later be a typical feature of this therapy, from now on moving on from crisis to crisis, owing to the ego weakness in this area of herself which Marion has actualized by her own drawings. In a week's time from now, the alarm she feels will reach such uncontrollable dimensions that she again has to be taken into hospital, this time as a day-patient for 4 weeks. Again she panicked, was unable to work or to be alone but returned home in the afternoon when her husband had arrived from work. As I worked in the hospital, the therapy could go on uninterrupted.

What can the drawings reveal of the underlying dynamics at this point of crisis? To come into existence as a separate individual might be a daring step forward compared with being nobody at all, crushed and depersonalized by the overwhelming mother image as had been her state in the psychotic area of herself. To evolve as a self might mean to leave a shelter because the emerging, orange, little person now again meets with the monster, re-experiencing the threat of being overwhelmed by panic. This may perhaps be analogous to the child's anxiety at being left unsupported by its mother at the time when differentiation normally takes place – causing it to be thrown back into undifferentiated fusion with its mother (Mahler, M. S. 1968).

31

The 4th hospital stay, from 28 February to 29 March 1965

7 March 1965

Here she is in hospital, and she has resumed drawing after having stopped it for a little while when her anxiety was mounting. Another typical feature of her drawing is seen for the first time: a severe challenge changes the structure of her drawings. From now on the compact monster, of which she had brought in all 18 versions, has disappeared with its unyielding, closed form. It has opened up, it now has an inside. It can be looked into and there is a possibility of being inside. It may reflect that a new mental space is now at her disposal.

Marion experiments and grapples with the problem of expressing how this is felt by her, and different solutions are seen in her drawings. Here the little person seems to be enclosed within the confines of the monster, captured inside it, while the flickering of the yellow-orange color seems to indicate anxiety and revolt.

I often got the feeling that her drawings emerged from the same level of psychic depth as do the myths and fairy tales. Somehow she now elaborates the theme of the little hero, standing up against non-human giants and monsters, involved in a struggle of life and death. After all, this was quite true psychologically at this point of time. Evidently a part of herself was coming into being which had been lost or perhaps had never really existed.

She hasn't yet much to say about these drawings, she isn't observant of the evolving process, nor am I. While the adult Marion speaks with me of her conscious difficulties in the sessions, she in her drawings unawares depicts a child, consistently and creatively ordering its experience. What we observe is the "bad mother" whose relationship with an emerging, struggling child is still repressed and undifferentiated.

12 March 1965

She is still in hospital. Her attempting to draw how "it feels" ends up with this structure of the relationship between the orange "me" and the earlier monster, which is now replaced by an abstract figure, an undefined "not-me" open to inspection. It is a sort of cave with red and black stripes for its walls. The "me", still in the process of coming into being, stands at the entrance of this cavity, looking into it. The first dawning of insight — the first suggestion of an observing ego.

She now defines the symbolic meaning of black and red, which are added to her color scheme and remain just as unchanged as the other colors. Black is sorrow and rage, red is her aggression, often connected with the fear of retribution, above all it is identified with her experience of hostile attacks and observations by her "neighbors". Violet and dark green invariably represent the hated and feared aspects of her all-bad, rejecting mother.

Sometimes the little "me" is drawn distinctly as a person, sometimes it deteriorates again and loses its human form. The light green surrounding this figure is also felt to be a very good color, also belonging to herself. What a big threat this little heroine has to face! However, she remains on her feet, stretching some good green tentatively into the cavity.

The therapist's gentle but constant and unyielding pressure on her to face her emotional difficulties is reflected in this drawing. Marion has internalized this request and elaborates it creatively, still quite unconsciously. She gives her associations to the colors but not to the situation, except for the notion that it concerns herself and her mother.

19 March 1965A

In hospital she soon remembered what had gone on in her before this actual breakdown. A girl on the job had reminded her of her half-sister Ellen. She had tried to suppress the violent emotions surging up in her by this provocation, only to fall victim to a return of her panic and depression. At that time I though this to be the whole explanation, and we talked of the futility of fleeing from the reality of her emotions. She was impressed by the lesson she had learned but, of course, the same sequence of events happened again and again – flight, followed by a flaring up of her anxiety. She hadn't yet the strength to cope with her stormy affects, and was easily overwhelmed by them.

Today I doubt that this version of her actual breakdown constituted the whole truth. Scrutinizing her drawings of this time, I – as mentioned – would rather put it the other way round: the beginning organization of a core of selfhood deep down in herself would actualize her fear and hate of the overwhelming object to which it stands in an inextricable relationship. There would again be a confrontation with the fear of annihilation caused by the very intensity of her affects. This cluster of reactivated fear and rage would be projected on to the very first, suitable person in her surroundings, as an externalization of the bad object.

In this drawing she is again captured within the mother-structure. She has lost her human form, but the good orange is expanding and stretches out like arms or wings. For the first time she draws the outlines of the "bowed snail" which will appear again and again, deeply hidden in the mother-cavity. For this snail she was never able to give any clearcut explanation. "It feels like this" . . . "it must be there" . . . Its secret – at least so I believe – will be revealed in the far later drawing of 23 June 1966 and the subsequent ones. I think it represents the hidden or at present still unrealized ability for a libidinal love relationship, irretrievably connected with her first love object, the mother.

19 March 1965B

Another version of the active, libidinal, stretching out into the mother-cavity. Marion's own remark to this drawing is: "I'm forcing my way into mother". A big tongue or phallus or probably an un-differentiated compound of both is observed in a sensuous search for unification with the desired mother. "I want her back".

This yearning for a full reunion with mother, this primitive urge to recover the precious closeness is, in my experience, one among others of the deep emotional motivations for the woman's wish to possess a penis. It often comes to the fore in the treatment situation. The mother has to be recaptured, even by rape, and the frustration rage adds to this creation of a phallic aggressive organ. This urge is more or less consciously displaced on to other women as a homosexual trend. I have seen this hungry craving typically manifest itself when there has been an early period of happy one-ness with mother that for some reason was ruptured before the child's development had enabled it to internalize the good mother as its own durable possession.

Marion's therapy seems to confirm that her disturbance is due to an early rupture of the libidinal tie to her mother, with its devastating effects on her further development.

Marion is at this time far from realizing this bisexual trend in herself. It will become conscious only toward the end of her therapy and then be accepted and integrated, and even illustrated as in the drawing of 28 September 1967.

Drawing by now has become a necessity to her; she makes one practically every day. For every drawing presented here there are about 6–7 others, elaborating the same theme, however, with a surprising richness of variations. The beauty of her drawings was quite unintentional. To Marion drawing only served her need to express herself, to find herself, and to communicate by its aid.

26 March 1965

In a few days now she will leave the hospital (29 March 1965). Her beginning individuation survives this first crisis. One may speculate whether the inner constellation, revealed by her drawings at this point of time, may be the typical one behind those unexpected relapses often seen in the treatment of psychotic or borderline patients who break down just when their therapist begins to note some definite progress. The relentless, internal persecutor comes to life in step with the emerging core of self to which it is irretrievably coupled, and the patient has no adequate defences against the actualization of this internalized bad-relationship. Probably the treatment of some patients with a psychotic core has to stop here, as further integration is beyond their capacities. They then have to rest content with the degree of improvement obtained by Marion prior to the drawing process, while the area of deep disturbance remains repressed.

After her discharge from hospital, Marion didn't return to her job, being too deeply involved with her therapy for the time being. Not till October 1966 was she again ready to resume it.

The relationship between the orange "me" and the "not-me" hanging over her has now become securely established, still a relationship of greatly uneven power. The little "me" is the searching one, stretching out her arms or some other symbol of self-extension toward something which isn't depicted as human, something located in the external world. Here the little person is wedged in between the stripes. "I can hardly move when they tighten around me like this". It is the observation by her neighbors, which is felt as squeezing and coercing her. "And over me is my mother . . .".

I was impressed by the intensity of her emotional involvement with her own drawings. As her therapist, my concern all the time was to counteract her tendency to flee from the pain of remembering and reliving, to evade it in some way or other. So I had from time to time suggested that she might also draw something she remembered. She had protested, shrinking away from recreating the past in such a direct way. But this day, in addition to the presented drawing, she brought her first pictures of two real memories. They were, however, so provocative that they were drawn in an almost invisibly pencilled line, unfit for reproduction. She sobbed when she presented them, telling me how awful it had been to let these memories emerge in herself. These pencil drawings returned several times, in between the "me" – "not-me" pictures, while she was immunizing herself against the almost unbearable pain of making them.

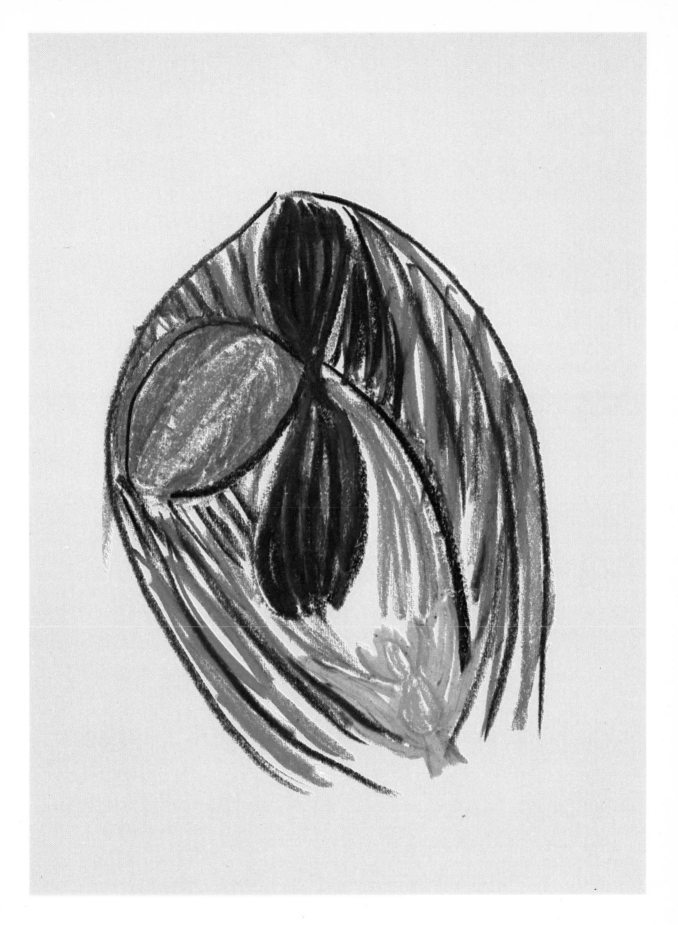

9 April 1965A

During two weeks of struggling with these memories the pencil lines gradually became stronger, but still there was no question of using color. Here these two themes, which appeared together from the very first time she tried them out, can be presented.

She is standing in front of the house where her mother lived with her husband and the newborn Ellen. A water pump is seen to the left. The striped square to the right is the window of mother's bedroom, where she nursed and fondled her baby. This window isn't visible from where Marion stands, it is on the opposite wall, but it is so important that she makes it hang in the air to include it in her picture. The house has no door, Marion is left outside; she is even separated from the house by a road.

Another memory of deep frustration is included at the same time (below). Marion is standing before the big fence surrounding the summer camp. However, to be sent away during the summer occurred also before Ellen was born. The feeling of being abandoned by her mother stemmed from an earlier time than Ellen's birth; the arrival of the sibling is associated to an earlier experience of rejection by her mother. In both pictures her reaction is seen to be identical. She is standing motionless, as if paralyzed. One feels the yearning, the loneliness, the utter hopelessness of expressing her despair. In the therapy she actually re-experiences the awful feeling of being completely cast out of the Garden of Eden. She is abandoned by her mother and is unable to react.

43

9 April 1965B

To confront herself with and recreate such intense suffering was a major task. The orange girl has grown by this challenge, and the dreadful, all-bad "not-me" hanging over her, loses a little of its compactness. Affective energy is visibly drawn from this "not-me" representation when some personal memory is reinvested with its appropriate emotional intensity.

What Marion projects into her drawings is, of course, all of her own psychic structure. It is the split in her we observe, between an emerging core of the self and the conflict area, the latter being dissociated from herself as a "not-me" and experienced as fraught with danger and threat. This area comprises both her own primitive emotions (sorrow and rage), represented in black and red, and her image of the rejecting mother, symbolized in violet and green. Thus the whole "not-me" area is made up of a condensed and undifferentiated compound of symbols, representing herself and her mother, split off from her emerging self and experienced as representing all her symptoms. It can in fact, be conceived of as the psychotic part of herself which, during the therapy, will be differentiated and integrated as a conscious reliving of the frustrating relationship with her mother.

I would here suggest that the drawing process, in combination with the relationship to the therapist, takes Marion back to the area of the "basic fault" (Balint 1968), to the early phase of her own development when the mother relation still is an integral part of the child's ego (Mahler 1968). Marion now actively confronts her bad mother-image of earliest childhood, erstwhile split off from the maturational processes and thereby having retained its archaic, terrifying quality. It was the very same bad mother who surfaced during the time of puerperal depression, at that time giving rise to the manifest psychotic disorder. So far, Marion has already collapsed once in the process of reliving this early fault in herself.

9 April 1965C

My dating of her drawings mostly refers to the day when she brought them to her weekly sessions and commented on them. After the session I wrote down her remarks to the drawings, in addition taking some notes as to her actual condition and on the main content of the session, Marion always presented her drawings in the order she had made them during the week.

The last but one of this week's drawings was this one. She is seen to turn away from her mother's house, which was never given a door, moving toward a house with a door, so far away that she has to turn the paper to express the distance.

The point of fixation, the paralyzed position, is given up when it has been experienced and relived with full emotional involvement. Some movement has become possible.

She isn't yet fully conscious of this herself. The drawings often hinted at a development to come, reflecting her first unaware projection of a deep impulse to change. It was easy to see more than she saw herself. However, I didn't want her to experience drawing as a threat of being seen through, before she herself was ready to face the message of her drawings in full consciousness. I was afraid to disturb this fine, spontaneous creativity, this process of finding herself through her visual imagery. My cautious attitude was not different from the sensitive approach to other emerging material in a therapy. Nothing is interpreted before the patient is close to the solution herself.

On the other hand, I had begun to use her drawings for the purpose of the therapy, in a way similar to that in which the child therapist will use the play constructions of the child patient. Both are intermediate means of concretizing the inner process, serving as a point of departure for the final verbalization. Later I shall sometimes intervene directly in the drawing process, just as the child therapist sometimes will actively move the toys to effectuate a therapeutic provocation.

9 April 1965D

Then the last of this session's drawings comes on the table. She has put her own good orange into the Marion who leaves mother's house. In the drawing on top she crosses out the good orange of mother's bedroom window. She can't bear to be reminded of mother's care for the baby sister. In the next drawing (bottom) she can stand it. The color of love shines from that window. Here, as in the foregoing drawing, the wall with the significant window is folded over to be included into the drawing, a typical feature of genuine child drawing. Marion stretches out her arms; there is vigor in her movement. She is released from her paralyzed position; surely she is here on her way to someone who cares for her. This person is always, of course, also the therapist. The patient's feeling of trust, of being understood and firmly held is the driving force of the therapy. But the therapist will fuse with the good objects of the past and reanimate them.

Is Marion on her way to her grandmother, to her house with a door for Marion to enter? Till now her drawings had entirely elaborated the image of the dreaded, hated and desired mother. I mentioned to Marion that the grandmother of whom she spoke so affectionately had until then never been seen in her drawings.

To my surprise Marion got extremely upset at the thought of taking grandmother into her pictures. She said it was impossible. Here was a clear demonstration of the fact that to talk of grandmother – which she had done freely all the time – and to recreate her in a picture, were two quite different kinds of experience. The act of drawing mobilizes a deeper level of emotional life than verbal expression, as Marion said herself: "...it all comes too near...I can't stand it...".

The defensive distance to something is lost when one sits down to the task of projecting emotionally charged imagery into a drawing. It is extremely provoking as one may try out for oneself. Some fleeting inner image cannot be pushed aside again, some thruth has come into being and is – sometimes mercilessly – reflected back to the drawer from the paper. Since I often make the adult patient draw – which is only possible when the child part of the adult begins to communicate directly with the therapist – I have seen how a drawing may release momentary fits of rage, of crying, of anxiety, of the immediate urge to destroy the drawing. The interaction that takes place between patient, drawings, and therapist is a powerful driving force toward integration.

48

Mourning in Love. 5 Drawings

16 April 1965

From 9 April onwards, when I asked about her grandmother, an intense drawing activity began, reflecting her attempts to master the released anxiety. From 9 April to 28 May – when a major change in the organization of her drawings took place – I received 56 drawings, many of them almost identical.

Around the central "me"-"not-me" structure, which remains essentially unchanged, there are disturbances and variations. Plenty of birds of flight are seen. The orange "me" is now a person, now a non-human snail. For this book I have to select a few representative drawings of the process involved. Marion herself was so disturbed, so tearful and anxious, that she was afraid she would have to go to hospital again. To this session she brings four drawings. In all of them her grandmother, drawn in colorless pencil line, is placed somewhere in the corner of the paper (bottom left). Here she sits by her house, friendly raising her arms. The orange "me" has collapsed and lost its human form. Two birds of flight reflect Marion's conscious urge to escape from something in connection with her grandmother. She can't explain what it is. She is so beside herself that she asks to be allowed to phone me between the sessions in order to hear my voice.

Grandmother had been Marion's constantly available, good substitute mother from the time of her birth and all through her childhood. Even though Marion may have had a tendency to see her grandmother as all-good in contrast to her difficult mother, her love for grandmother is so consistently present during the whole therapy that this relationship must have been a genuinely good one. In the drawings grandmother from the very first moment of her appearance is seen as a whole person, free from distortion, patiently waiting for Marion to find her. In comparison, Marion's mother announces her presence through the threatening monsters and in spots of bad colors, dispersed all over the conflict area.

23 April 1965

She brings nine drawings to this session, all of them elaborating the struggle that grandmother's appearance causes her. This drawing reflects the perturbation. The orange "me" has here deteriorated to a small, imprisoned snail. There seems to be a little crown on its head, however, indicating that something valuable – though yet unknown – is represented. The "not-me" masses are weighing heavily and threateningly upon this snail, which seems to need a fence to protect itself against the all-bad violet and green stretching out for it. A bird of flight is seen in the cavity. Marion herself appears far away at her mother's house (top left). She draws herself as the one who has gone wrong, unable even to locate the right direction for her search. Grandmother sits quietly waiting, her arms raised as if to receive her forlorn grandchild.

At the time of the actual therapy I didn't understand. Why is the snail imprisoned and seems to succumb to an impending, overwhelming disaster? Is the all-bad mother forbidding her to yearn for grandmother? I have asked my colleagues when I present the slides I have made of these drawings. Obviously it is difficult to come upon Marion's own answer. Thoughts go to hidden anger, repressed ambivalence, heavy guilt-feelings and so on. The impact of blocked mourning isn't always uppermost in the therapists' mind.

Marion is extremely upset, she is again on the point of breakdown. However, from now on a bucket is seen at the water pump in every drawing. It wasn't there before. Does it mean that Marion expects a container to be found for the streaming waters – for the overflow of her tears?

30 April 1965

The patient teaches the therapist, as usual. Another week of inner work brings the solution. In six of the eight drawings she presents in this session, the "tree of sorrow" has appeared (bottom left). Here a crying Marion is on her way to grandmother who stretches out her arms toward her (top). Both are still drawn in the tentative pencil line.

Marion had been unable to mourn when grandmother died, and grandmother had been completely lost to her after her death. There was nothing but emptiness. My question about her grandmother had disturbed Marion's repression of her affectionate relationship to this love object. This revival of their relationship – now a purely internal one – forces Marion to pass through the pain of realizing and mourning her loss. Her grief had been too overwhelming to be lived through.

But now Marion had gained access to her sorrow. "The tree is what is dead and cold in me ... Something in me died when she was dead ...". The warm orange overflows the cavity; the snail has no defensive fence around itself and has grown in size. The orange little person has returned, now drawn with a resolute certainty and is quite clearly a little girl (bottom right). It was with these drawings that it dawned upon me for the first time that this girl had developed out from the first orange worm. I laid out all her drawings – in all 49 – after each other for the first time, and we looked at them together. There had been a steady, gradual, slow growth of this orange self-representation throughout all these drawings. Marion was somewhat surprised herself but not really impressed. "Oh yes", she said, "this is just that new part of me which has become able to look at the disaster ...".

An orange bird is seen within an enclosure (middle right). In some of the drawings the spruces around the fence betray that this drawing symbolizes a representation of Marion in the summer camp.

7 May 1965A

Here Marion stands quite close to grandmother (bottom left), but there is still no color in this group. Both have raised their arms, however. An orange bird of flight is seen in the cavity into which the snail too has retreated. In our sessions it becomes evident that Marion still tries to defend herself against this developing contact between herself and grandmother. When grandmother died, Marion was just frozen, without any feelings – the dead tree.

To open up again for her love and at the same time realize her loss, is to invite suffering. When one is dead, nothing hurts. Marion cries, finding it quite impossible to cope with her awakening love and yearning for her grandmother. However, the mourning process proceeds in spite of her resistance.

The orange girl, the onlooker, from now on remains on her feet in every drawing, never again losing her human form.

Another Marion moves decidedly away from mother's house (top left).

Marion is not fully aware that what she draws stands in utter contrast to what she consciously experiences. In our sessions she faces the despair of the loss, suffering an agony almost exceeding the limit of her endurance. So while Marion struggles with her overwhelming sorrow, "detaching her memories and hopes from the dead" (Freud 1917), she all the time draws herself as approaching grandmother. At a deeper level the mourning is clearly conceived of as a reunion, a mutual stretching out for the lost relationship. The process, as Marion depicts it, seems quite natural to us. The chosen symbol of death, the dead, frozen tree, serene and beautiful, also conveys the impression of something natural. "Something died in me when she was dead . . .".

7 May 1965B

Here is a later drawing from this week's homework, reflecting the ongoing process. While Marion is despairing in her tearful anguish, overwhelmed by sadness and grief, her hot tears seem to melt the frozen love. This again bears a certain resemblance to the fairy tales where something lost and frozen is called back to life through the hero's compassionate tears. Here there is a beginning revival of the affectionate relationship between herself and grandmother, again depicted as a mutual process. The good orange of love is filling out both of them; soon the miracle, promised mankind in its fables, is going to happen.

The orange snail deep inside the mother-cavity again wears its little crown. I ask what this snail means. Again she answers: "It has to be there . . . it is something in me that is dejected and lost, somehow . . .".

The orange, confined bird (middle right) has for some time appeared in her pictures. It is a non-human aspect of Marion. In this retrospective scrutiny of her drawings every non-human representation is seen to denote something that is still undifferentiated and repressed. Here it heralds the next conflict to be worked through, the sibling jealousy. Marion was in the summer camp when she received the letter from mother, telling her of the birth of Ellen.

13 May 1965

Marion arrives at this session, overwhelmed by happiness. She tells me that a miracle has happened. Grandmother has become alive and has spoken to her. Marion has heard her mild voice and is able to clearly recall her looks. Grandmother is quite near. To the drawing she says: "Grandmother and I have now to be drawn in yellow, it is a good and calm color (bottom left). She supports and encourages me. She was always so kind to her own husband and children. She advises me to be like that toward my own husband and child, and then I'm able to treat them like *she* did ... When *she* says that my child is a darling, I can bear close contact with Lillian for some little time ... I feel closer to my husband too, but there is still very little sex ...".

Yellow represents a new quality in her emotional life, a tranquil, quiet trust and security. It is added to her color scheme, and its meaning remains as fixed as the other colors.

The mourning process has made the love of grandmother available to Marion, that is, her own love is freed to be invested in grandmother's image and all the good memories connected with her. It has an immediate effect on her real life. For the first time since her breakdown three years ago, she gains some genuine hope. She feels that somebody loves her, and this gives her the rich feeling that she herself has something to give. The love in this relationship, which till now had been lost, can at once be transferred to her own family. It is impressive to watch how this support from an internalized love object from her childhood is felt to exceed any support she might get from her therapist and her husband. The orange snail radiates beams of love. Surely this snail has something to do with the deep joy of refinding a love object.

Here the mourning process presents itself as something intensely painful, but in essence uncomplicated and natural; it is a bitter necessity to go through it in order to regain the love that had once been invested in this relationship. Marion's love and gratitude seem to pervade even the suffering. Here is no bitterness, no rage for being abandoned, no ambivalence, only a deep despair at the loss. This is in utter contrast to the other mourning processes Marion has to go through.

The bird in the summer camp has changed into a coal-black Marion (middle right); a tail or a penis is added to denote her dangerous qualities. The stripes at once tighten around the onlooker, indicating that this rage is partly projected onto the "neighbors" who are always felt to keep watch on and control what goes on in Marion.

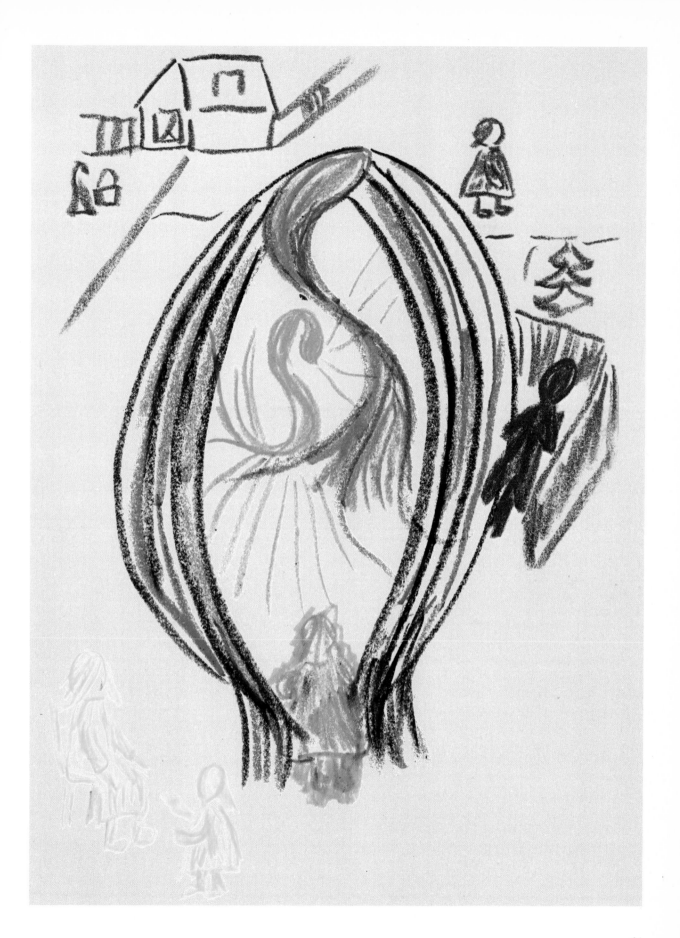

61

28 May 1965A

There are 15 drawings between this one and the former, all working over the same theme. It was after a visit to town by her half-sister Ellen that Marion had to draw herself coal black. Marion couldn't even tolerate a telephone call from her without feeling the most intense hatred and jealousy. During the sessions she had now ventilated much of her rage against Ellen. I had then remarked that Ellen wasn't seen in the drawings. Marion had reacted with a violent protest: "There is no place for Ellen in the drawings . . .", as there of course had been no place for Ellen in her emotional life when she was a child. Again it became evident that to talk of Ellen and to admit her presence in the drawings were two quite different kinds of experience. What appeared in the drawing was acknowledged and had to be accepted.

Here she can stand the fact of Ellen's existence. She has appeared at mother's house, behind a fence (top left). Marion is frightened at the immediate growth of the black girl (middle right). The support of grandmother is now a constant feature of her daily life, and the yellow group appears in every drawing (bottom right). Marion doesn't feel totally abandoned any more. However, the presence of Ellen makes the drawings more dangerous; Marion is again anxious and depressed, afraid not to be able to bear this new provocation. The neighbors are felt to observe her so keenly that she again has difficulties in leaving the house. All the same, the orange girl firmly keeps her position and observes it all. Through the inner work of mourning she has become definitely individuated as a little girl. The drawings may serve as an illustration of the complexity of the psychotherapeutic process. One conflict area after the other is reactivated; whenever a solution is found, a new cluster of undifferentiated emotions emerges to be cleared up. So far, there has developed a part of Marion which is able to observe herself. And she has gained access to a lost love object. The "not-me" is definitely thinned out by this process of differentiation. The pictures also tell us, however, that the mourning as well as the now available, internalized love relationship have all the time been placed in the periphery of the drawing. Centrally we find the still non-human symbols of mother and illness, indicating that the primary problems are to be found here.

28 May 1965B

From the first drawing of 6 February 1965 to these ones of 28 May 1965, Marion had needed 111 pictures to develop her various themes; 21 of them are presented here, those left out are all variations of the same constellation. There is a central "not-me" representation, conceived of as situated in the world outside. It was all hanging over her, subduing her, squeezing her. Thus there had been till now a split between the developing observer and what she observed, while both in fact were representations of Marion's inner reality. However, the whole area of conflict had been dissociated from what she conceived of as "me".

There now comes a shift in her inner dynamics, quite spontaneously depicted in her drawings after I had subjected her to a great challenge.

Marion had drawn the black angry figure in the summer camp 21 times; it had grown constantly bigger and was clearly identified as her own bad sibling jealousy.

In this session I proposed that we take the black Marion out of her confinement to see what this rage was really like. During our talks she had still been quite unable to express any emotions directly. She could only report this rage; what she felt was anxiety and depression. Marion was hesistant about taking the dangerous step of removing the fence around this figure. She proposed trying it out in my presence. I gave her my prescription block and she made three small drawings:

a. She attacks Ellen behind her mother's back. At the same time she clings to grandmother for support.
b. She tramples Ellen down to the earth, annihilating her.
c. She is left behind in utter misery while Ellen and mother go away.

These drawings at once became intensely real to her. Now that her rage was set free, she became afraid of the risk of hurting Ellen. So I proposed that we might lock up Ellen in the cage in the meantime to protect her. Marion is very relieved by this.

Till now mother had been felt to be the all-bad mother who had persecuted and abandoned her unhappy child. Here Marion's own destructive rage and the ensuing punishment of being shut out is depicted. There is a beginning realization of her own "badness" at this deep level of experience. Probably it is the unfailing love of grandmother that gives her the strength to accept this rage.

8. The Furious Bird. 9 Drawings

4 June 1965A

At home, Marion tries to work out this new situation in her drawings. The released rage is too intense, however, to be expressed and handled by the person Marion. She is unable to contain this rage. What had been the coal-black person in the summer camp – and, for a very short time the little girl destroying her rival sibling – now seems to explode (top) and be lifted up into the air, weightless with rage. Ellen is safeguarded by being locked up.

The exploding person develops wings and a tail (bottom) and places itself over Ellen in the cage. The impulses of rage are again depersonalized and relegated to an area outside her ego organization. Marion hasn't yet the strength to express them as her own personal affects.

She takes refuge with grandmother, who loves her even though she is bad (bottom right and left).

I had a motive for this provocation. Ellen, now 17 years old, was living in the country with relatives. She had already borne a child and was being helped to care for it herself. However, she planned to come to town in the autumn of this year to go to school here. This threw Marion into an abyss of despair. She and her husband were well off, and it would be impossible, not to take some care of the lonely Ellen. Ellen was rather uninvolved in the sibling conflict and was fond of her elder sister. Marion was aware of this and this increased her own misery. She felt Ellen to have the power of destroying her life.

The therapy had to help Marion to differentiate between the object of her destructive childhood envy and the unassuming Ellen of today.

4 June 1965B

There is no time for color while she struggles to achieve a new equilibrium. The rage can't return to the safety of its confinement in the camp. A bird is found to be the right symbol for these destructive impulses, which remain hanging in the air above Ellen, who is seen to tumble under the impact of this radiating fury. But she is safe, so far.

It is good to have a quiet place with grandmother (bottom right). Marion had till now projected her own destructive impulses into the outer world and then perceived them as hostile attacks by her neighbors, whom she imagined to be observing her. These impulses are now taken up into herself and acknowledged as her own, though yet out of contact with her central ego organization.

It is worth noticing that when a peripheral figure in the drawing, the black Marion in the camp, was set free, it completely changed the central concept.

Her very relationship to her archaic mother-image is deeply affected. Rage toward a sibling who is in reality quite harmless is, after all, only a displacement of her primary rage against her mother, who is believed to have given all her love and goodness to the sibling.

This again reflects a characteristic of the psychotherapeutic process. The working through a more peripheral conflict opens up for changes at the very heart of the disturbance.

For a long time the sibling relationship will take over the fundamental conflicts with her mother, this relationship, however, slowly becoming pervaded by mother's bad colors. Marion is able to direct all her fury against her half-sister, reliving it in full consciousness. To direct it against the mother herself is as yet not possible.

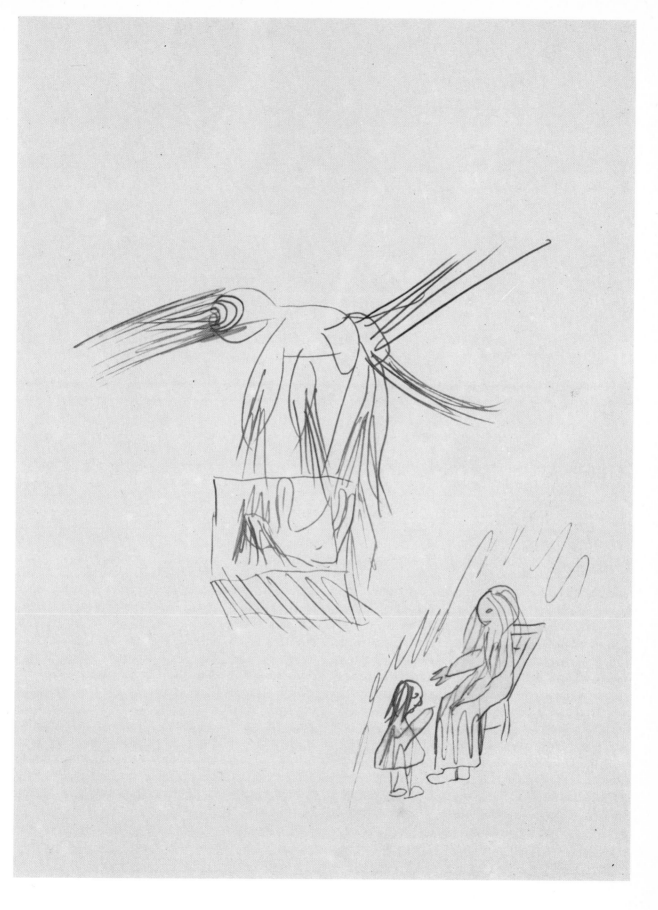

11 June 1965A

The effort of handling these intense emotions results in a fundamentally changed structure of her drawings. Some of the colors have returned here, but the central "not-me" structure has disappeared and will never return. It is replaced by the bird, which Marion acknowledges as belonging to herself. "It is awful to be aware of it inside myself, but somehow it feels better . . .". Both the observer, who has also gone for ever, and what she observed, have united in the furious bird. The bird has here taken over the black and red stripes identified as all the world's hostility and especially as the threat from the neighbors. Here it is beyond doubt Marion's own aggression, the bird having developed directly out of the destructive little girl. Also the good orange and light green from the former on-looker find representation in the bird. "It's tail tries to reach grandmother . . ." (pencil lines). However, in these first drawings of the bird the ominous violet and dark green are left out, the colors of the all-bad mother.

There is no more dissociation; by reliving and accepting the rage, an important step toward integration has taken place. During the following 10 weeks (4 June to 20 August 1965) in which 58 drawings are needed to elaborate this new constellation, the furious bird will hang over the fenced-in Ellen. This fence is a magic one, preventing Ellen from being hurt by the fury, even though the bird's evil intentions make her fall down from time to time. A light blue is here tried out as a suitable color for Ellen.

The love relation to grandmother is again drawn in the good, calm yellow. Marion has to some extent composed herself after the excitement of this restructuring of inner forces.

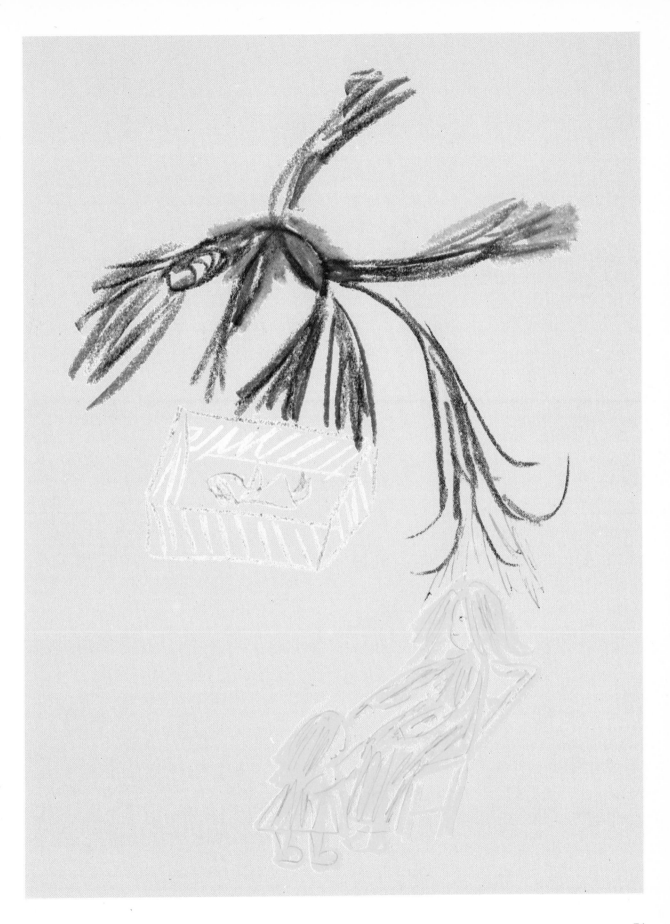

11 June 1965B

Or maybe Marion should try to give Ellen the good, yellow color. She is after all innocent of having been born. Marion now seems to struggle to separate her half-sister from the destructive conflict with her mother.

In these first pictures of the bird it seems to bite into something. I mention that the bird has something in its mouth. Marion replies that it is a sort of yearning, the bird stretches out for something. Black, here seen in the bird's mouth, is, however, the color of rage.

We are justified in suggesting that these drawings indicate the oral level of the conflict, that is, the conflict belongs to Marion's early infant relationship with her mother. Of this she yet knows nothing.

18 June 1965

The violet and dark green, now appearing at the bird's head, at once make the drawings more dangerous. Marion feels worse, she is very anxious and again has difficulties in leaving the house. Everybody looks straight through her. She wonders if she can stand having that bird inside herself at all.

For support another group is taken into the drawing, here tried out in pencil lines. It is her husband with whom she takes refuge (bottom left). The third person is her daughter Lillian (bottom), seen to be of the same age as herself. Lillian is standing aside, as she does in real life too. Lillian at this time is three years old.

I ask Marion what goes on in the bird. She answers: "It wants mother". So it is a bird both of desire and rage – or, in more professional language: both of libido and aggression – represented by the corresponding colors, orange and red-black. But the bird has also taken up in itself the representation of mother, through violet and green. Thus the bird is again a condensation of some repressed relationship between Marion and her mother, containing both of them.

25 June 1965

The yellow color for Ellen won't do. Inevitably she too – just as the bird's head – acquires the bad violet and green. It is impossible at this time to differentiate her from the mother. She is supposed to have stolen Marion's good mother and to have preserved this good mother inside herself. She is the target of Marion's most destructive jealousy.

This change, however, makes the drawings more dangerous; Marion's anxiety is mounting, but in the process of working through her rage, it clearly diminishes again. The fury of the bird threatens her supporting groups too, indicated by the black and red stripes over her husband's head (bottom left). This family group of real life has now acquired the good yellow color, to Marion's own great satisfaction. The big orange tail of the bird also comforts her. "... it is something new and good ...". The tail is from now on drawn without elements of black color.

There is a consistent ordering of experience to be observed, at this time comprising a splitting process through which Marion struggles to separate the good from the bad. So far, she has succeeded in diverting the aggression from the bird's tail. A part of herself feels good.

After some abreaction of her rage, Marion can report a certain improvement. "Everybody says I'm changed ...". Now and again she is able to feel close to Lillian and then keenly experiences what it would be like to really mother a child. But then Lillian again "changes into Ellen", making Marion feel all bad and desperate.

Seemingly Marion has a relationship of just the same quality both to her husband and to her grandmother. It makes no difference in inner reality that grandmother is dead. Lillian is always left standing apart from the supporting groups (bottom). At this time the whole family leaves the town for the summer holidays. Marion dreads the autumn when Ellen will come to town.

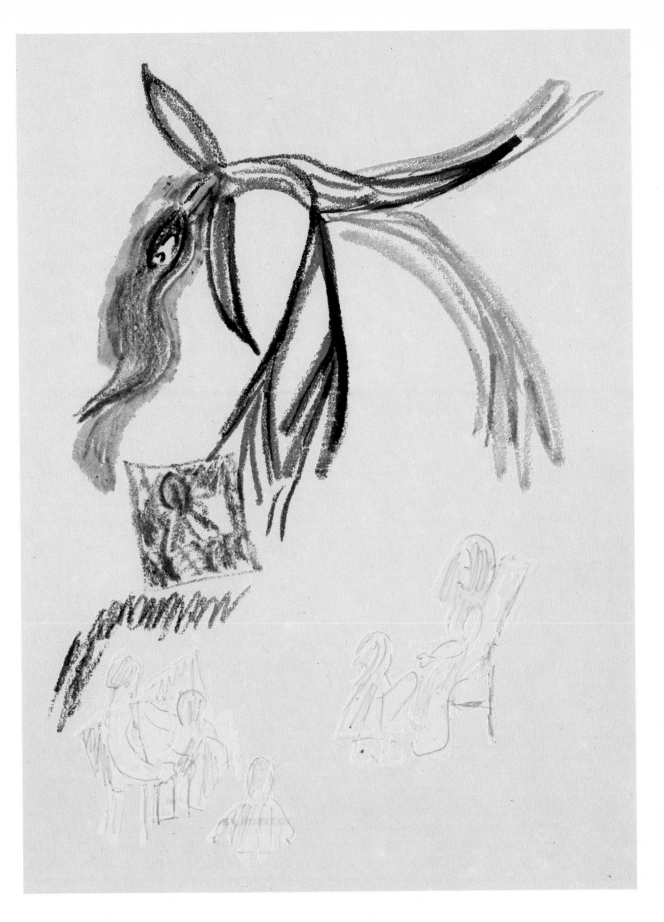

6 August 1965

After the holidays we continue the therapy. Marion has had an urgent need to draw almost every day during the vacation. "It is the only way to feel like a real person . . .".

She brought 22 drawings, almost identical with this one presented here. Among the holiday drawings, however, there were three tiny ones in colorless pencil line, in which she had tried to take Ellen out of her cage. "I wanted to try it out, but I got so upset that I had to put her back into the cage. I didn't want to spoil my holidays . . .".

Ellen has grown during the summer; in all the drawings her head is above the edge of her confinement.

I had from time to time made some remarks about the loneliness of this bird that Marion knows she has inside herself. Somehow it is far away, speaking to no one, just bursting with a rage that is never directly expressed. Marion tells me that it is impossible for this bird to have contact with anyone. She has tried to draw fine pencil lines from its good tail to see if they might reach grandmother. But it won't do. She was never able to tell grandmother how she felt about mother and Ellen. Marion is still the compliant woman, just telling *about* this fury inside that makes life so difficult, causing her so much anxiety and depression.

In a few weeks now Ellen will settle in town. Marion is desperate. She sees no possibility of coping with Ellen's presence. Ellen grows in her cage.

The bird radiates its fury towards her supporting groups.

13 August 1965

But Marion must be able to endure Ellen's coming to town. She will arrive in just a fortnight. So I propose that she takes Ellen out of her cage. After all, Ellen will move about freely in town. Marion says she will try. And she does.

But at once she loses control over Ellen, who grows into a huge, threatening being. The whole supporting world shrinks disastrously. The therapist is now added to this group, acquiring the same good yellow color of support (at the top of the yellow groups). Marion now has to protect her supporting relationships by a demarcation line. "... between the good and the bad ...". This line is drawn in orange, the color of love.

All the supporters, however, are outweighed by the power of Ellen. Marion is overwhelmed by anxiety. Her whole world is in danger. Ellen, in the all-bad violet and green, is seen from behind. Beside her is her child, drawn in a pencil line.

80

9. The Subhuman Figure
18 Drawings

20 August 1965

To take Ellen out of her cage meant to disturb a defence mechanism. The inner work necessary to face and deal with this anxiety situation again results in a shift in the representation of the conflict area. A more human-like figure, already seen in some pictures of 13 August, spontaneously replaces the bird, which will never return, as is always the case when her representational scheme alters. This figure is still no real person; it has taken over the bird's diffuse head with mother's evil colors. It is also of a motionless stiffness, as if frozen. But some humanization has taken place. We may suggest that the conflict area has drawn a little nearer to the area of integration, to the ego organization.

However, it is still quite out of contact with the rest of Marion and with her good relationships. Fury radiates toward the overwhelming Ellen. The supporters are small, indeed. The therapist is now given a place of her own (top right).

A struggle starts between Marion and the therapist. Marion maintains that the evilness of Ellen will destroy her life; she thus organizes herself along paranoid lines. The therapist reformulates this: Ellen makes Marion feel so bad that she is afraid her life will go to pieces because all goodness may disappear. Ellen, now seen as a threatening persecutor, causes an upsurge of such destructive impulses in Marion that they have to be projected back onto Ellen.

A thick line of demarcation is necessary to protect what is left of her good world.

The child of Ellen escapes the bad colors. A little act of love by Marion?

27 August 1965

For the next three months – with the aid of in all 86 drawings, of which 18 are presented here – Marion will represent the main conflict area by this little sub-human figure without a distinct head. The supporters are all invariably depicted in the calm and even yellow color. The hot passions of love and rage belong to the other side of the demarcation line, symbolized by colors of quite another intensity.

Marion makes drawing after drawing of the all-powerful Ellen, who shakes her existence. I again induce Marion to take a further step toward reality. I suggest that this huge sister, always seen from behind, might not be identical with the real Ellen coming to town. What if Marion turns her around to see her face? Marion, after some anxious hesitation, manages to do so, and at the same time starts to encage this subhuman figure, at first with fine pencil lines. Lines of demarcation between the good and the bad are still necessary.

I had gone on with my remarks about the loneliness of this little figure. What if it tried to communicate with someone among the yellow supporters? Marion can think of no one who might wish to make contact with such evil. I say that I understand a lot about how angry children feel. I suggest that I might stretch out an arm.

So I appear in the drawing with one arm stretched out – in the opposite direction to the isolated figure as an illustration of Marion's resistance.

The yellow world has slowly recovered. Marion's own child always stands alone. Marion is still unable to be a mother.

3 September 1965A

Marion struggles through the crisis brought about by the blow of Ellen's appearance. Here she has to some extent restored the balance of powers, Ellen and the therapist can almost match each other in size. The little subhuman figure, now radiating some good orange, is resolutely framed.

By so doing, the demarcation line has become superfluous. Marion mentions that it was a dangerous step to take "because it is more *one* world now . . . It is more dangerous to live in, but it feels better . . .". Marion seems to be somewhat milder. Ellen is no longer enveloped in the radiating fury from the little figure, and Ellen's child has been given the good yellow color. A certain peace seems to prevail. But Marion has begun to cry in her grandmother's lap (bottom right).

To this session Marion brought five drawings, her homework during the week. She laid them on my desk in the order she had made them. The first three are almost identical with this one, the therapist is seen to raise her arm in the direction of the little figure. After presenting this one, No. 3, she suddenly told of a dream about a witch. Angrily she says that the therapist is a witch too, forcing her to suffer, unwilling to help her at all, bringing her no relief. "I'm afraid of you. All the time I have just complied with your wishes."

Till now she had not told me of any dreams. This one and her comments express rage and revolt directed toward the therapist. This is something quite new; till now she had been the compliant Marion, mainly uttering her protest and anxiety in the form of begging for some new tablets that would alleviate her suffering. Her anxiety that I will abandon her when she betrays such aggressive feelings flares up immediately.

The yellow color of the therapist suggests that she till now has been placed with the supporters, to all of whom Marion has a clinging, helpless attitude.

3 September 1965B

Then she puts drawing No. 4 on the table. The hand of the therapist is seen to penetrate the figure's frame, which here again is almost invisible. A flash of aggression radiates from the figure's one foot. I grasped the meaning of this sequence of events. I tell Marion that I think I have guessed the secret of the little figure. It is furious with someone it also likes and is dependent upon. She had during the last sessions begun to complain about feeling herself inside a glass house, unable to get out. She felt all locked up, isolated, unable to express herself. She was becoming ever more aware of some isolated entity within herself.

In this retrospective study of Marion's drawings one might speculate at which level people with analogous early conflicts tend to stabilize themselves, eventually with the aid of a therapy? Perhaps here somewhere? Conceived of in terms of object relationships the siutation might be commented on like this: the core of deep conflicts (the subhuman figure) is encaged, that is repressed, controlled. The mother herself is invisible. The bad internal object, now represented by the sibling, has become tolerable. Life goes on among good enough, supporting relationships. This inner situation of relative order may be typical of what supporting therapies can achieve with sufficiently good result. The situation may also approximate to a typical basic configuration of internalized relationships in average normal people, as this psychic organization tends to remain relatively stable when there are resources to control or repress the "bad side". But the even yellow color betrays that something is lacking in these good relationships. The vital colors of rage and love attached to the primary objects of childhood aren't represented here. That vitality is locked up in the "bad-me"–"bad-object" relationship which remains isolated. Also, an infantile Marion seems to cling to her supporters, taking shelter with them against the threat emanating from this unintegrated bad aspect of herself.

Maybe Marion would have been able to achieve stabilization at this level of maturation. Certainly many therapies ought to halt *here*, since a great challenge is ahead for those who venture further. In Marion's case, however, her many relapses had convinced me that stabilization would not be possible until she had mastered her conflicts. I also believed in her possibilities of growth. This explains my rather bold insistence on that she should go on struggling. I actively stretch out for the withdrawn part of herself, which now seems to be available. I certainly didn't realize at that time what it would imply to break through the major defence of an "ego-weak" patient, to penetrate the very wall of schizoid withdrawal.

3 September 1965C

Drawing No. 5 comes onto the table. A black hand has broken through the frame, clutching the therapist's hand. I felt relieved; the contact was established.

To my consternation, however, the further unfolding of this situation meant a castastrophe, an unmanageable crisis of psychotic dimensions. This will be the second situation of danger in this part of her treatment into which she is impelled by her own drawings; Marion again has to be hospitalized.

The very break in the protecting wall, the very contact with the isolated core of herself, caused an immediate re-experience of the trauma of object loss, of abandonment, transferred onto the therapist and the whole outer world. The paradox arises that this very contact of necessity means an instantaneous loss of it again, a rather bewildering situation for the therapist. The good therapist now seems to disappear from the patient, who collapses in despair.

Such a situation is aptly described by Fairbairn:

"At the same time there is now little doubt in my mind that the release of bad objects from the unconscious is one of the chief aims which the psychotherapist should set himself out to achieve, even at the expense of a severe transference neurosis, for it is only when the internalized bad objects are released from the unconscious that there is any hope of their cathexis being dissolved. The bad objects can only be safely released, however, if the analyst has become established as a sufficiently good object for the patient. Otherwise the resulting insecurity may prove insupportable." He points out that "when such an escape of bad objects occurs, the patient finds himself confronted with terrifying situations which have hitherto been unconscious. External situations then acquire for him the significance of repressed situations involving relationships with bad objects". (Fairbairn [1943] 1968) pp. 69—70.)

Marion, at this point of her therapy, is going to illustrate with surprising accuracy the clinical situation caused by the "release of the bad object". The severe transference neurosis has already manifested itself through the flaring up of Marion's anger towards the therapist.

11 September 1965

The evolving crisis confronts the therapist with an unforeseen situation.

Marion arrives at this session, crying helplessly, afraid of becoming mad. She is extremely anxious and disturbed, and asks me to send her to the hospital for ECT-treatment. The neighbors are everywhere, following her with their hostile eyes. Her black bad hand has become visible, and she feels defenceless. She tells me that some days ago she learned that Ellen had changed her plans; she wouldn't come to town this year. After a flash of relief, she suddenly felt that she had lost everything, all contact, there was nothing but emptiness. She adds that Ellen reminds her of the most painful part of her mother. She obviously isn't able to differentiate between Ellen and mother, and she now seems to experience the loss of her object. She brings six drawings with her, and in all of them the contact is lost again between the black hand and the therapist. She tells that she has desperately tried to make them meet, but they won't. Her hand is dirty and bad, nobody wants to hold it. In this drawing the hand has five real human fingers groping for contact. Her anger with me, heralded by the dream of the witch, continues to find expression. I'm locking her up, unwilling to help her. She expects immediate retribution, that is my withdrawal from her because of this anger. When she becomes convinced that I can stand her rage without punishing her, she calms down a little, and we agree that she continues with her psychotherapy. I give her some more medicine to help her stand the crisis and work it through.

I was bewildered. Why do not the hands meet? The drawings all look rather peaceful. Ellen is of a bearable size, nothing new threatens. However, Marion's tears in grandmother's lap have yet to be explained.

Marion's excitement does not subside in spite of medicine and extra sessions. A complicated state of affairs is initiated, which soon becomes beyond her capacity to handle. What emerges from repression is the bad object, the very mother herself, experienced in the transference through Marion's anger with me and her expectation of losing my support. But it was more than that. Good memories of her mother suddenly come to the surface. Marion remembers how she lay in bed with mother, enjoying the warmth and closeness. She yearns for the time when she was living with mother and Ellen, regretting now her own unkindness towards them. Today she would have taken more care of Ellen. She plans to make some garment for Ellen's child. Her hate is suddenly replaced by ambivalence, which, however, seems to tear her to pieces. She vizualizes Ellen standing in her sitting-room at home, sneering at her: "Your unhappiness serves you right". Angrily she says to me: "Often I see *you* standing sneering at me in just the same way".

I remark that I haven't got any of the bad colors even though she feels I'm sneering at her. When she answers that this would be far too dangerous, we are able to talk of the pain of hating someone of whom one is also very fond.

The 5th Hospital Stay, from 17 September to
19 October 1965

16 September 1965

Her husband has phoned. Marion's excitement has become unmanageable. He asks for more medicine to calm her down. I refuse, proposing he should bring her to an emergency session, and she arrives, extremely upset, putting this one drawing on the table. She sobs violently, bangs on the walls, shouting that she hates me for my power to release all that is painful. She would have never agreed to a therapy if she had known what suffering it would imply. She can't stand it any longer, she wants to die. She feels all imprisoned without any hope of liberation. But she is also enraged, shouting that she sees her mother and Ellen all the time. When she has calmed down a little, she is somewhat ashamed and wonders how she will manage to behave herself at home. I suggest that she should come to the hospital as a day-patient for some time while we work through the present crisis. She agrees and is hospitalized the next day, her 5th hospital stay.

Later in this session she comments on her drawing. Her black hand has again got hold of another hand, after seven days of desperate groping in the empty air. On top she has contact with Ellen, below with her mother, both appearing in all-bad colors. They are drawn quite identical, Ellen is not distinguished from her mother. So here was the explanation of the last week's struggle: Marion is now unable to reach a good, supporting object. The "bad-me"–"bad object" relationship is at last exteriorized as a very real experience. Here there are no contact difficulties. The black, bad hand belongs to a corresponding bad object.

For the first time her mother appears as a whole human being in the drawings. To the left she is seen again: drawn in pencil line she stands with her angry, dangerous eyes; the bad, frightening mother herself. Marion, in corresponding pencil line (below), cannot stand the sight of her and falls down. An exact and intuitive illustration of the clinical picture. The release of the bad object has at the moment become too much for Marion.

All the same, in spite of her panic, the atmosphere of the sessions has changed completely. There is regret and guilt, a wish to repair, an ambivalence where also mother's good aspects have come into being. Till now there had been mainly rage and persecutory fears. In the Kleinian frame of reference such a clinical picture would probably indicate that Marion is on the move from a paranoid-schizoid to a beginning depressive position. It was all started when the symbol of her schizoid detachment, the defensive wall of the subhuman figure, was broken through.

Depressive Mourning
12 Drawings

25 September 1965

Her therapy, now characterized by Marion's developing experience of the abandonment by her mother, continued in the hospital setting, from now on with sessions twice a week. This drawing indicates that not all of mother has appeared as a whole human being. The non-human mother-bird has returned, in entirely bad violet and green, seen hanging over a little, black Marion (top). The meaning of this split-off symbol accompanying her conscious depressive mourning, remains repressed and unconscious for the next seven months. It will then reveal itself as the lost, early mother of symbiotic one-ness (drawing of 23 June 1966). Maybe Marion, in fact, genuinely illustrates a passage by Freud (in Mourning and Melancholia St. Ed. vol. XIV p. 245): "... the patient is aware of the loss which has given rise to his melancholia, but only in the sense that he knows *whom* he has lost but not *what* he has lost in him. This would suggest that melancholia is in some way related to an object-loss which is withdrawn from consciousness, in contradistinction to mourning, in which there is nothing about the loss that is unconscious".

Beneath this mother-bird an interesting situation

appears. A crying yellow Marion in a more mature representation of herself than hitherto – thus in full accordance with the clinical picture – is again able to find the therapist's hand. However, the therapist now appears in all-bad colors, identical with mother and Ellen on the foregoing picture. There seems to be just *one* bad object. The negative transference, here establishing itself, is necessary in order to relive and express the repressed rage, resentment and despair, which have now broken through. This yellow Marion appears in three drawings, then disappears, just as the severe depression sets in. She seems to communicate that she is handing herself over to the therapist, yellow being the color of support and trust, while at the same time she is depicting the inevitability of the negative transference. Marion's preconscious knowledge, guiding both her and me through this therapy by the creation of her genuine symbols, is indeed remarkable.

A quite tiny Marion is seen, isolated in a play-pen, all colors gone (middle right). The subhuman figure has withdrawn its arms and has lost every trace of the good orange (bottom).

96

1 October 1965

Marion's excitement and acute persecutory fears soon gave way to the full unfolding of a severe depression, and, after some time, she consciously mourns the loss of her mother's love, re-experiencing it through the trauma of her mother's marriage. It is abandonment, despair and yearning which are lived through and illustrated. The "terrifying situation" (Fairbairn 1968), which had hitherto been unconscious, is returning from repression and experienced as real. The external world is changed into a world of only bad objects, including a bad therapist. The colors of her drawings fade. As all her supporters are seen to have disappeared we may also for this reason suggest that Marion not only relives the situation when she was nine years old, but also regresses to a far earlier time when mother really meant all the world to her. Till now the situation of being completely unloved and abandoned had only existed in her internal world, comprising the relationship with her bad mother-image.

In her drawings Marion appears as an insignificant little person, rejected by everyone. The loss of mother's love and the loss of self-esteem are seen to be different aspects of the same trauma. In a lot of drawings she wanders on endless, desolate roads in her veil of sorrow (middle left). The unkind therapist behind her desk refuses to help, and Marion – depicted as empty and depleted of color – is stretching out for the telephone, for contact. A black Marion stretches out for the mother-bird with an identical gesture. The negative transference is experienced in a very real way, the therapist has become the actual bad object.

A new theme has appeared, mother and Ellen in bed together, enjoying their bodily closeness (top left). This is a sight that mobilizes Marion's most furious and agonizing jealousy, while at the same time it heralds that her own yearning for the goodness of her mother is drawing nearer. Again a loss of a love relation is mourned, but – in contrast to the mourning of grandmother – this time there is no uncomplicated refinding of a lost love object. The anger at being betrayed and deserted will soon manifest itself. Something starts radiating from the arms and legs of the stiff, subhuman figure.

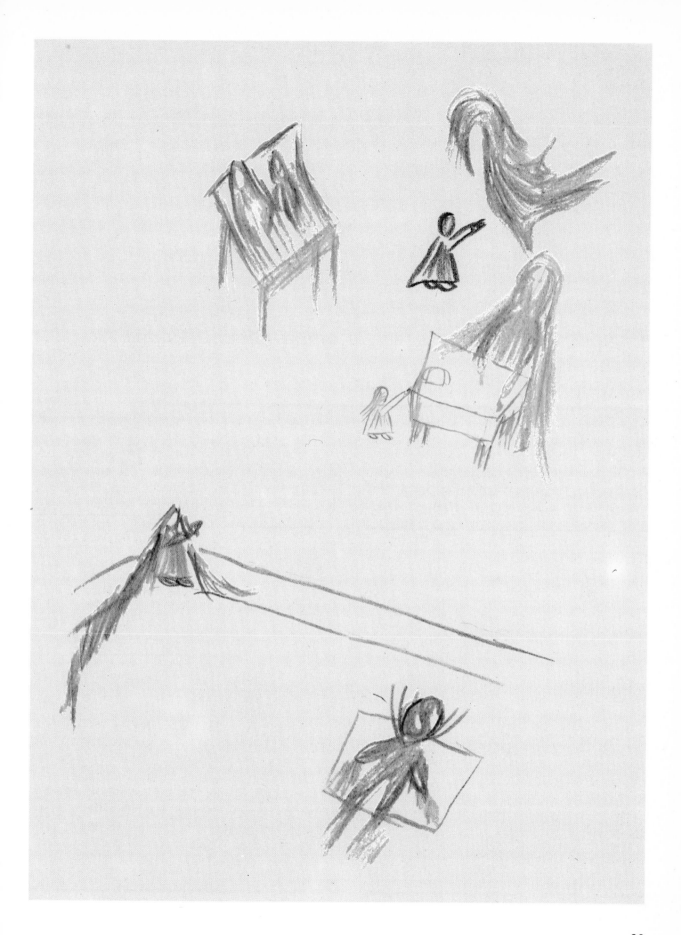

9 October 1965

After three weeks in hospital Marion feels able to leave. Her therapy has survived the crisis. Today is her last day as a day-patient. She has been drawing all the time, and her pictures reflect a gradual change. The subhuman figure has again broken through its frame, first with one arm while here the other penetrates the frame. It has grown and gained more freedom of movement, reflecting the abreaction of Marion's intense affects. However, she still has to draw herself in the deep pit of depressive despair, unable to climb its walls. Over her hangs the mother symbol, weighing her down (bottom left). This symbol is in its form identical with the head of the subhuman figure. This is no mere coincidence; a still unconscious relationship exists between those two symbols, between Marion and her mother, to be worked out later in the therapy.

In the upper, left corner, a frightening, all-bad therapist is seen, a stick in her hand. Marion, to her right, is small in comparison. However, her begging, helpless attitude seems to be gone, the colors of rage are tightening in her. The therapist's stick may reflect both a need for heightened control and an expectation of punishment.

Marion in the upper right corner develops in a way that frightens herself, scratching at the bed where mother and Ellen lie together. During the session Marion feels these impulses in her own hands and is afraid that she might lose control over them.

Marion is now so pressed by her emerging aggression that from now on she will have sessions twice a week as an out-patient until the summer holidays of 1966, and from then on again, once a week. Despite severe crises to come, she will from now on master them without having to be rehospitalized.

The reaction to the loss of a love object is described as typically consisting of three phases: *firstly* one of yearning, protest, and rage. The bereaved is still fixated on the lost object and displays an angry urge to recover it. *Secondly* there follows a period of despair and disorganization, hope being given up. *At last* there comes a phase of reorganization of the personality, partly in connection with the image of the lost object, partly in connection with new attachments (Robertson 1953, Bowlby 1960, 1961a, 1961b). However, a loss is sometimes too overwhelming to be mourned. Instead of reorganization there comes detachment, that is a repression of grief, rage and despair, and the lost love relationship is not regained in internal reality, in the way we observed this process through Marion's mourning of her grandmother. We are going to observe how close Marion's own experience comes to this model of mourning.

18 October 1965

So far, Marion's detachment has been given up, symbolized by the black hand breaking through its frame. The despair of being abandoned is lived through. Now the repressed protest and rage emerge, Marion displaying the furious urge to recover her mother. Here Marion's hands have reached Ellen in bed, while the ominous mother-bird watches her ill-doing from behind. Now that she has laid her hands on Ellen, she becomes afraid that she might do the same thing to her own daughter. It is still difficult for her to differentiate between the reality of today and the tempestuous affects of the past.

Both arms of the subhuman figure have now penetrated the frame; they seem to move freely, and both hands have fingers. Marion is becoming ever more aware of the impulses in her own hands, and the urge for affecto-motor release is pressing upon her.

A quite new group is seen (bottom left). Marion tells me that her grandmother has returned, with her mild voice and face. She had been all gone during the weeks of abandonment and depression, and Marion had been unable to recall how she looked. Now Marion is at once feeling better and hopes that grandmother will stay with her. The essence of Marion's depression (and probably of most severe depressions) was her feeling of profound worthlessness, of being abandoned in a world of entirely bad objects, with all love and goodness gone. Here goodness returns, as indicated by the good yellow and orange colors. Marion has drawn a group of three generations. To the left sits grandmother, in the middle Marion herself. For the first time she appears grown-up in comparison with her child (right). And for the first time she takes Lillian's hand. The warmth from grandmother passes through herself to Lillian. Marion has matured through the suffering of her depressive state.

Another characteristic of the depressive state is also here clearly demonstrated. The released deep core of rage – Marion's own, at first unbearable, badness announced by the black hand – does not simply become abreacted. In between lies the depressive mourning, calling the object of this rage, her deserting mother, back to internal life. Initially Marion can only experience herself as the helpless victim of this emerging, all-bad mother, the mother who abandons her child when it is still in need of her. Only slowly will she be able to integrate and express her own badness as really her own frustration rage.

22 October 1965

Marion in black and red — still with her veil of sorrow — is steadily growing. Here her hands pass across Ellen and stretch out for mother. The subhuman figure has freed one leg from its frame and moves wildly. Marion's own impulses to scratch, hit, and trample have at this time become so urgent that we have to arrange for a release during the session. For the first time she lies down on the couch, however, only for the last, half hour. I want to be sure that she doesn't isolate the therapy with its emphasis on inner reality from her real life. To flee from all that is painful is still a major tendency. So during the first part of the session we continue to sit face to face, and she tells me about her daily life, about her conflicts with others, about her feelings and experiences. This arrangement continues during the rest of the therapy reported in this book.

In this session she tells of a dream in which mother appeared so good and kind. But then Ellen was present too, and Marion felt wild with rage. She yearns for and hates her mother; her ambivalence is overwhelming her. Lying on the couch she cries and shouts — bangs her fists and yells, afraid of losing control altogether. The intensity of her emotions is reflected in the subhuman figure. In one of her drawings at this time again a glimpse is caught of a more mature state. Here she sits as a mother, taking the hand of her child, without needing the immediate support of her grandmother. "I felt like this for some little time on Sunday". However, most of the time she is afraid she might harm Lillian and sometimes feels that she has actually done so. Only with great difficulty is it possible for her to tolerate this explosive destructivity now surging up. Angrily she demands of me that I shall relieve her, she has suffered enough, how long is this misery of hers going to last? The neighbors are observing her all the time, she is unable to stand it all any longer. She is anxious and depressed, needing my firm, holding support to be able to accept the reality of her own state.

The earlier yellow supporters never reappear. They belong to a past stage of maturation serving at that time as a protection against the split-off relationship with the bad object which Marion hadn't yet been able to face. Now Marion has confronted this bad object and is re-experiencing her own bad self.

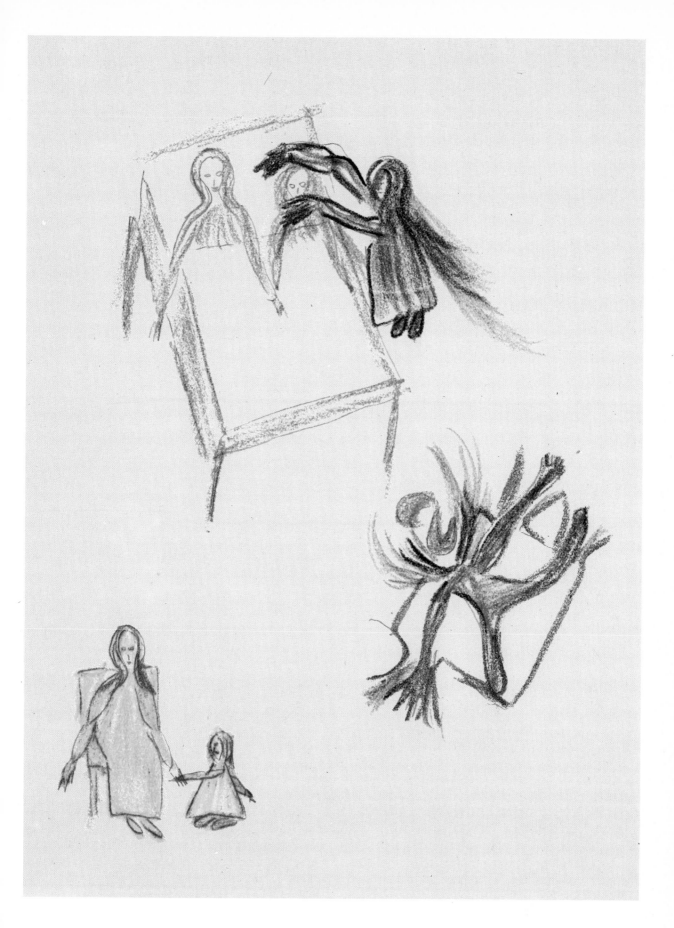

24 October 1965

In spite of all her verbal complaints, her drawings unfailingly reflect the process of differentiation and integration. Here a memory has been actualized, so intensely painful that it has to be drawn without color. She is in the summer camp and has just received the letter from her mother telling her about the birth of Ellen. She had felt crushed and utterly miserable but had pretended to be proud and happy and had danced around with the other children, the letter in her hand.

She feels that she has been pretending all her life since that day, hiding her real emotions. There is a slowly growing awareness in her of her compliance and of her fear of not living up to the expectations of others. In the picture she is seen from behind. She isn't yet able to face this pretending girl.

26 October 1965

Marion, who with growing rage has reached out for her mother, here for the first time tries out a solution of her conflicts. So far, it is an attempt at reorganizing her relationship with her mother, thus representing the eventual end phase of the depressive mourning process. Her comments to this drawing are that after all she did have something in common with her mother – they both took care of Ellen. Here they both stand enjoying the sight of the pram with the newborn darling. Marion, however, still carries her veil of sorrow, and both mother and pram are drawn in entirely bad colors. Marion and her mother are separated from the pram by a thick line of demarcation. The baby is not seen, and Marion has no eyes. The solution doesn't quite convince us.

It is about this time that Marion suddenly understands why she has chosen violet and green for mother's bad colors. Ellen's pram was green. Mother wore a violet dress at her wedding.

The more Marion's hands approach her mother in bed, the angrier she becomes with me. She accuses me of withholding my power to lessen her suffering. Time and again she demands more drugs, more ECT treatment, renewed hospitalization. I interpret that this is exactly how she felt about her mother. Her mother too was felt to withhold her power to help and soothe Marion in her despair. Now Marion is demanding to get access to her mother's goodness.

It is observable how Marion, through the abreaction of her hate and jealousy, in reality comes closer to the good memories of her mother. Correspondingly the subhuman figure slowly acquires some good orange around its neck, representing the still latent capacity for love.

7 November 1965

Marion grows steadily; here her long arms have reached her mother. The negative transference reaches its climax. In paroxysms of rage she shouts that I'm a hag and a witch who forces her to go through a suffering like this. It is all the therapist's fault now. I order her to be locked up, I refuse to set her free. She can't stand it, she won't be obedient any more, she will defy me and not comply with my wishes. At the same time she feels terrorized by the neighbors who look right through her, even through her windows and walls. The pent-up revolt and aggression causes an intensification of her persecutory fears and even more intensely does she experience the fear of being abandoned by me. The other aspect of her ambivalence also reaches a peak in intensity. She remembers the feeling of security, of quiet trust when she lay in bed with mother. She has asked her husband if she might lie quietly in his arms without any sex, explaining to him why she yearned for this. She had experienced a blissful state of security and wellbeing in his arms. It had been ages since she had felt anything like this.

However, she feels her yearning for mother as something intensely painful, with her rage intervening all the time. She cries, kicks, bangs on the walls, shouts out her agony. Sometimes she sees her mother as a skeleton or a ghost, searching for Marion, and then Marion pities her, but refuses to be found. This vision of her mother frightens her. She is so torn by her ambivalence that she is unable just to make a report about it. In her violent affecto-motor discharge reactions she seems to be flung between the extremes of rage and love.

In this drawing the subhuman figure has both its legs out of the frame, an illustration of the liberation of Marion's affects during the sessions. The good orange color is seen around its neck. Marion still struggles to solve her conflicts by trying to identify with mother's happiness with the newborn Ellen. There is still no baby, Marion still doesn't look at the pram.

110

111

12 November 1965

Marion's power and strength to express her violent rage is reflected in the ever bigger Marion. No good color reaches at this time the actual persons in her drawings; they remain depicted in their purely bad aspects as their colors involuntarily betray. On another level, her struggle to achieve a reconciliation continues; now she has got rid of the demarcation line isolating the pram from herself and her mother. Still no baby, however. In fact, Marion looks as if she wants to sell us this seemingly satisfying solution (bottom right).

When she lies down on the couch, after the first half hour of verbal interaction with me, she plunges, without the slightest hesitation, into the internalized relationship with her mother. Mother's presence, looks, and actions are so vividly vizualized – and described – that I often feel the three of us to be present. When in her rage she wants to punish and hurt her mother, she immediately "sees" her mother's threatening face and often cries in agony as she feels she is being beaten up by her. Then there is a change, she sobs and gently strokes the walls and the cover of the couch, remembering mother's soft skin, her hair and good hands. All the time she is angry with me for not being able to relieve her from this suffering. She is, however, feeling more secure that she will not be abandoned by me and therefore feels more protected generally. She tells me that the walls of her home seem to thicken when she feels more safe, and then the neighbors cannot observe her.

The raging affecto-motor storm constantly takes on new nuances. After an outbreak of rage against me – of an intensity that really shocked her – she had seen her mother's face with a kind expression and had heard her voice saying: "I don't wish you to be unhappy". Marion thinks this is too good to be true, and the heavy pressure on her by the internalized bad mother lessens a little. She discusses with me if there might be a possibility for her to wear some gay clothes. This had been felt to be forbidden. At other times she rejects the advances of her mother. She had dreamt that mother invited her to lie in bed with her. Marion had then said that she wanted to stay with her grandmother. She is rather desperate about the complexity of her own attitudes.

112

113

15 November 1965

In this drawing a new personification of Marion has made its entrance. She tells me that the little person in front of the house with all the windows is her daily self, going out shopping before the eyes of the supposedly hostile neighbors, a rather difficult task.

She can now link up the pretending girl from the summer camp with the pretending Marion of today. She always makes an effort to appear as a contented and happy housewife and mother. She vaguely feels that this is the reason why she always feels "criticized and looked through".

Through many drawings now, it has become manifest that Marion is unable to look at the – non-existent – baby in the pram. Here she has no eyes. She doesn't succeed in identifying with her mother's happiness with the new-born Ellen. This is a solution found by many children, but Marion cannot achieve a restructured relationship with her mother and half-sister at this level. The task of mourning the loss of her mother is still unresolved. Mother and Ellen are still drawn in completely bad colors, betraying that no restoration of the love object has taken place. In fact, the solution she tries out coincides with the appearance of the "pretending" actual self in front of the neighbors' windows.

What this depressive mourning has in common with the former mourning of her grandmother is, however, something rather important for Marion's further maturation. Here too, there has been a thawing of something frozen and stiff, till now represented by the immovable, subhuman figure armoured behind a wall of detachment. There has been a release, not of love, but of repressed despair and frustration rage, which have been openly expressed and integrated, symbolized in the drawings of the subhuman figure now slowly freeing itself from the imprisonment.

19 November 1965

The subhuman figure, the heiress of the furious bird, now freely swings its arms and legs. So does Marion on the couch. Her body and mind have to a larger extent become one whole; all of Marion expresses herself through weeping, shouting, banging and kicking, and then again through gently caressing the walls and the cover of the couch. I had the definite impression that she found her own body during these sessions. I could observe how her respiration deepened after these outbursts, how her voice became full and rich. Afterwards she immediately felt more real and alive, in spite of the pain. I felt that her pent-up emotions, now liberated, were being integrated into a psychosomatic, whole self, a process that must have been halted during an early stage of development. This period of the therapy was essential in order to bring her out of her subdued, compliant state – out of the very depersonalization she had suffered for so many years. The "framing in" of the subhuman figure had thus symbolized the blocking of her own, authentic emotions from loco-motor expression, while the "breaking through" represented the newly gained possibility of releasing them again within the safety of the therapeutic relationship. This amounts to the birth of a "true self", of an ego not dissociated from genuine bodily expressiveness, replacing her "false, compliant self" (Winnicott 1975 [1950]). Her affective storms had nothing of the hysteric's flight from some insight or from verbalization through acting out. On the contrary, I kept up a constant demand on her to verbalize what she was experiencing in her semi-hallucinated state on the couch.

Of this picture she says that she feels stronger and bigger on the street when going out shopping, not so haunted by the neighbors' observation.

116

10. The Controlled, Dangerous Girl. 18 Drawings

21 November 1965

Marion has abreacted on the couch during 12 sessions, from 22 October 1965. The figure has broken through its frame, but its head is still mysterious and diffuse with its good and bad colors, indicating that something is still repressed and outside the area of integration. To this session Marion brings four drawings, all elaborating her earlier themes. I mention that we have by now become very well acquainted with this subhuman figure, which has expressed its emotions freely for weeks. I wonder if it still has to hide its head. Both its rage and love are entirely human. Hasn't the time come for it to be drawn as a human being? However, this is felt to be such a dangerous step that Marion proposes to try taking it in my presence. Again I disturb a defence mechanism by directly interfering with her drawings, since I have judged the situation to be ripe for this sort of intervention. Her identification with her drawings is so complete that I can communicate directly with the child in her through entering into her mode of structuring the drawing. It is again parallel to what the child therapist sometimes does with the child's play constructions.

Marion sits down to draw in my presence. What emerges is a girl with a big, aggressive, greedy mouth. Marion becomes frightened by her ugliness, and partly to control her, partly to support her, she places this girl between the therapist (to the left) and the mother (up to the right). This girl at once kicks away the hated pram. She becomes aware of a new dimension of her aggressivity, and the immediate result is the falling apart of the former ideal of being her newborn rival's nice big sister.

For 7 months and 160 drawings this impulsive girl will stand in this position, firmly held by both her mother and her therapist, who are drawn as being quite identical. A very concrete illustration of the transference situation. As is usual with dangerous drawings, they at first have to be drawn without color.

26 November 1965

The subhuman figure never reappears. A new scheme of self-representation has taken over. The appearance of this girl, however, causes such an anxiety crisis that I have to give her some extra sessions. Marion must now face her destructive rage at another level. There is no longer an obscure head which made it possible to keep her hatred at some distance. From now on she has to take full responsibility for it. The big mouth and the teeth again betray the oral level of the conflict – it belongs to her early relationship with her mother.

Biting impulses at once come to the fore, actualized and made conscious by the new arrangement in the drawing. Marion, lying on the couch, makes a ball of her woollen glove and bites fiercely into it. The accompanying imagery is vivid and frightening. Above all, the fantasies and impulses are felt to be really her own. She bites Ellen "till her blood comes", and her former death-wishes toward her are recalled. When she wheeled Ellen in her pram with the nice, obligatory smile everyone expected from her, she secretly hoped for a snowdrift to fill the pram. Or maybe Ellen would be suffocated by her straps.

She explains this drawing where the colors have returned: she feels herself to be very dangerous and in need of being held. She kicks and tramples on what she hates, the pram and the bed with mother and Ellen. The therapist, always sitting to the left, and the mother up to the right both have their good and their bad side, as indicated by the colors. In the first drawings of this new situation, Marion herself is drawn in the colors of pure aggression, in red and black.

With this new upsurge of destructive impulses she again becomes increasingly haunted by the hostile condemnation of her neighbors and appears here rather small before their windows.

The full expression of her ambivalence toward her mother continues all the time; mother sometimes appears good and mild, wanting to help Marion on, but then again she is stern and punishing. "All in all she is more friendly."

17 December 1965

Lillian had now began to develop symptoms. During the late fall of 1965 the kindergarten staff had become alarmed by her condition. She appeared depressed and withdrawn and had frequent fits of masturbatory activity when she would lie down on the floor, regardless of her surroundings. Lillian had been referred to a child therapist and had begun her treatment. Marion understands that Lillian "hasn't had her mother" and from her own treatment she knows what that means. While later she became integrated as a loyal cooperator in Lillian's therapy, she had first to work through her rather complicated feelings in connection with it.

Her actualized frightening impulses to bite and kill, associated with the visualization of blood, are inevitably transferred from Ellen to her own daughter. She has, however, the strength both to admit and to control these urges. Her impulses to strangle Lillian and to cut her throat are abreacted in the therapy. We have reached the very core of the typical puerperal psychosis, the urge to destroy the child. However, Marion clearly feels how much stronger she is becoming through the conscious experience of this murderous rage.

There is also another aspect of having got a big mouth. She reports that she has for the first time been able to defend herself against the criticism of her mother-in-law by giving her a sharp reply. Till now she had always reacted with unhappiness and inferiority feelings toward her mother-in-law, hoping in vain for her approval.

After 17 almost identical drawings, this one introduces a new theme. On top small objects have appeared. Those to the left are the toys of her half-sister, which Marion formerly had to put in order. To the right are Marion's actual household-utensils. She is equally annoyed with both, her ambivalence is spreading to every aspect of her daily life.

Marion now draws herself as a mix-up of orange, black, and red, a true picture of her inner state. Below, Marion going shopping has again gained in strength by accepting and partly abreacting her violence. I had suggested that in front of the windows Marion should stop acting as if everything were in order. She might just as well admit that she had difficulties too, just as everyone else had their troubles.

Marion accepted this. The neighbors are allowed to guess that there are difficulties. She relaxes and is not so afraid any longer. "I'm getting stronger when I admit how it is . . . ."

10 January 1966

Marion indeed needs the firm grip of her two guardians. All her rage and envy are intensified by the appearance of her aggressive mouth, above all the envy of her own daughter. Lillian has a father, a mother, a kindergarten, and now she even has a therapist. Marion is also afraid of losing Lillian to the therapist. Her relationship to her child is at this time extremely labile; Marion is torn between her frightening, murderous impulses and her sudden feelings of genuine tenderness. When, for a short while, she has been able to cuddle Lillian on her lap, then her own feeling of bereavement and bodily hunger returns and with it a mounting rage. No doubt, the very core of the puerperal psychosis has been approached. However, when the real Ellen paid a visit to town at Christmas, Marion was surprised that their meeting wasn't so difficult any more.

In this picture the toys (top left) have changed into Lillian's toys. Marion is fed up with her household duties. She feels imprisoned in a dull and futile existence, and angrily demands of me that I set her free. She wants to take a job, to have fun going out with her husband, to buy some smart clothes. It all is forbidden to her. That was just the way her mother enjoyed her life, and Marion hated her for it, accusing her of being a bad mother. Marion cannot bear being like her mother.

Nothing prevents her from widening the scope of her life in this way in reality. Her husband, who from time to time comes with her for a joint session, would be glad if she did. She even considered a part-time job at this time, but was unable to solve her ambivalence. "My mother forbids me to be happy and independent, to take a job. The neighbors (her persecutors) deny me the right to be at home as a housewife because Lillian is at the kindergarten." Marion had needed a medical certificate to obtain this accommodation for her daughter, which as a rule was only granted to working mothers. In this drawing Marion, however, for the first time appears with Lillian in her lap (bottom left).

125

7 February 1966

Marion brings her drawings to our session; all of them are practically identical. Here there is again a spontaneous change. The struggle with her overwhelming ambivalence has made her strong enough to relive her destructivity in a quite direct way. This drawing – too dangerous for color – introduces the new situation. The newborn Ellen in her pram has become visible for the first time (top left), and Marion looks straight at her. When this scene appeared some months ago, Ellen was invisible and Marion had no eyes or looked away. That this is a danger situation is reflected by the immediate change of the therapist into a witch with a long nose and a broom. The firmly held Marion seems to be the very illustration of the weeping and gnashing of teeth. Never has her mouth appeared so acutely dangerous (middle right). The crying Marion in the summer camp, mother's letter in her hand, permits us now to see her unhappiness. There is no pretending any more.

The non-human symbol, the bird, the split-off and unintegrated aspect of her mother, again enters the drawings, having for some time stayed in the background. The last time this mother symbol was seen in the pictures presented here, was in the drawing of 18 October 1965, where it watched the angry Marion from behind. From now on it again acquires the definite form of a bird and is always seen in a fixed relationship with Marion, from now on for a long time sitting with her child in her lap somewhere in the drawing. The integration of this relationship between "Marion-the-mother" and this bird is as yet to come; at this time it is still repressed. It is again the unfaithful mother of the nine-year-old Marion who is now confronted and punished by her deserted daughter, this time with the full acknowledgement of her own destructive rage.

11 February 1966

The therapeutic setting is the same. During the first part of the session Marion sits up, speaking of her conscious conflicts and experiences, giving me a clear picture of her actual state. When she gave up taking a job, she was haunted for weeks by the following ideas already mentioned: "The neighbors", supposed to be intensely envious of her being a housewife with kindergarten accommodation for her child, "forbid" her to dispose of her time as she wishes to. She feels compelled to stay indoors all day long. At the same time she is in a rage against her mother, who "forbids" her to take a part-time job, to enjoy a greater independence. Mother forces her into the drab life of a housewife because Marion as a child had been so angry with her working mother. Marion's compliance with the imagined demands of others is striking. Her own genuine needs have no rights of their own. To differentiate Marion's and her daughter's situation today from the past one between Marion and her mother is a task requiring much time and support.

During the last part of the session, with Marion lying on the couch, her deeper conflicts are released and freely abreacted. This drawing deepens her rage and sadness. "Everyone expected me to be glad when I got a sister ... I hadn't had enough of my mother myself ... and my mother whom I loved so dearly ..." Then again she experiences the terrible urge to tear Ellen to pieces, to bite her to death. Marion loses all zest for life, feeling she has no right to exist when this overwhelming badness of hers emerges. "And Lillian, my own kid, has to pay for this ..." Marion has no distance to this pain. She cries, hits, bites, tramples and sobs on the couch, then quietens down with a deeper respiration and an acknowledged feeling of being more whole. The drawing depicts her grief. Her tears are streaming down when she angrily reproaches her mother (middle) or stands with mother's letter in her hand. "Marion-the-mother" under the bird (top) appears unconvincing in her yellow and orange colors, compared with the forcefully drawn Marion below. The mother–child situation (top) seems to represent a wish or a vision of the future rather than a real state. Marion tells that for some brief period she is "a whole mother to Lillian" but then her own bereavement and intense jealousy intervenes. The bird too has here some good orange, reflecting that the positive side of Marion's ambivalence slowly gains momentum.

18 February 1966

Marion's two controlling supporters have lost every trace of good color, Marion is in a rage against both. The therapist is depicted with her long nose and her broom, the witch herself. During the sessions Marion accuses me of holding her back, forcing her to live her dull life. The negative transference is complete, it is all the fault of the therapist. As Marion, however, never fails to appear for her sessions, she somehow knows better. It is a question of exteriorizing her bad internal relationship with her mother onto a safer and more predictable person, the therapist.

On top are the symbols of her imprisonment, her household duties. All three Marions cry in this picture. She explains that her actual self (bottom) and the girl in the camp both are the suppressed and the submissive ones, having no rights of their own. They are just complying with the expectations of others. Everyone expected a smiling face when her sister was born. There was no one to talk to about her misery. Today everyone expects her to be a contented mother and housewife with no reason for complaints. Marion realizes the identity of her actual self with the unhappy pretending nine-year-old she once was. This is reflected in the drawing. The shopping Marion (below) and the girl with the letter both appear in identical grey and red colors, both are crying their hearts out.

130

131

28 February 1966

This time, however, there is a therapist to whom she can tell of her misery, which is now approaching its very peak of intensity. Her rage-sorrow-yearning-murderous urges are relived and abreacted through the affecto-motor discharge reactions. Mother's punishment is directly experienced in the sessions as being beaten up. At the same time a deep wish for reconciliation again comes to the fore. She wants to cry out her sorrow in her mother's arms as Lillian should cry out in her own arms. "I have the same feelings toward my mother and my daughter." She is jealous of Lillian's male therapist and wants him for herself as a father. She admits it quite shamefully along with the flaring up of her rage against me for not satisfying her hunger for a mother. The beginning revolt against the pressure of her internalized, stern mother – projected on to me and on to the "neighbors" – is expressed in the following way: "On Sunday I defied you all and went to the movies in the afternoon".

What disturbs most is the way her own child is drawn into the internal struggle. Lillian is mixed up with her half-sister in an alarming way. "And I who have always been so fond of children – I always looked forward to a child of my own."

In the drawing "Marion-the-mother" appears small and unreal under the big bird, while the frustrated Marion watching her mother with the newborn baby has grown in size. There are no good colors in this mother–child group. Marion at this time says: "Before I'm able to be a mother, something else will have to happen first ... I must be allowed to grow up myself ..."

She is excessively paranoid in the midst of her revolt, feeling keenly observed by the neighbors. Something is stirring in her but is not yet fully accepted – the neighbors regularly know about it before she herself does.

6 March 1966

The developing drama takes place between Marion's mother, caring for the newborn Ellen, and herself watching this scene. In between these drawings there are other pictures of herself, in the firm grip of her two supporters, indicating that the situation is under control by the therapeutic setting. No acting out occurs at home, Lillian is not in danger. Marion needs much time and many drawings to struggle through her own destructive envy, which is experienced as having so direct a bearing upon her own capacity to be a mother. A spontaneous change is seen in "Marion-the-mother" as the result of our work. She has become more real, there is more substance to her body as she sits under the sway of the bird (top).

The child Marion watching Ellen on the bathinette looks like a brewing thunderstorm, just before it bursts into lightening and thunder. Something is going to happen.

She again feels small and guilty in front of the windows of the neighbors.

135

13 March 1966

It is no thunderstorm but a firestorm that is now breaking; Marion's destructive rage has reached its climax. Mother and Ellen are cast into the flames and are destroyed by fire. At the same time Marion is so disturbed by this wave of murderous urges that I have to promise to take her into the hospital as an emergency case, if necessary. The Easter holidays are approaching, and she fears this break without contact with me. However, as the drawing reveals, she can bear to look at the fire.

On the other hand, it becomes evident that the experience in full conciousness of these impulses makes them less dangerous. The distance Marion had to keep to her child, diminishes by and by. Marion can draw herself as an actual mother in ever more dynamic colors. There is a growing mutual identity between the various personifications of Marion in the drawings. Lillian is still unreal.

It will be seen that mother and Ellen in the flames are represented in their purely bad aspects, as indicated by their colors. They are the bad, pain-arousing objects that have to be destroyed; Marion struggles to get rid of their oppressing influence on herself. Her own forceful activity now undoes the traumas she once went through, then as a passive, depressed and lonely little girl.

In real life her relationship with Ellen is now very different from before. She visited her sister in the country three weeks ago without any difficulties.

The situation, erstwile initiated by the black hand breaking through the wall of detachment, is seen to have developed into the long drawn out process of dissolution of the cathexis of her bad objects, just as described by Fairbairn (see drawing of 3 September 1965), Marion's rage is abreacted and the bad objects are cast into the flames. Again in Fairbairn's words: "It becomes evident, accordingly, that the psychotherapist is the true successor to the exorcist, and that he is concerned, not only with the foregiveness of sins but also with the casting out of devils" (Fairbairn [1943] 1968, p. 70). That is, the "devils" – the bad objects – become exteriorized, and their power lessens in step with Marion's open expression of her hate, fear and her wish for aggressive retribution.

31 March 1966

The storm rages in drawing after drawing. Marion destroys Ellen and her mother in the flames, in essence a symbolic act of punishment to conquer back her own autonomy and independence. Her first terror-stricken reaction to this misdeed by and by gives way to a grim glee of putting an end to their power over her. Here she burns up a painful memory. She had once been invited by her mother to spend the Easter holidays with her and Ellen in a cottage, only to experience the deep disappointment of feeling left out by them. She does away with this memory (bottom).

Passionate hate has warmth in it, after all it is derived from her frustrated love. The flames seem to lighten up the whole drawing. Marion's two supporters have regained their good side, and the bird radiates more good orange. "My mother is much closer, she wants to embrace me but the flames are between us . . ."

Much vitality had been tied up with this repressed frustration-rage, and its release gives Marion more freedom of imagination and gradually lessens the burden of her guilt. At the top of the drawing there now appears a vision of a happier future. Marion sees herself as a contented mother with a new baby (top left). To the right she and her husband go out to amuse themselves. Till now her hatred of the well-dressed mother who went out in the evening to enjoy herself had barred Marion from realizing such wishes in herself. Grandmother, flat-heeled and modestly dressed had always been at home as a good, caring, substitute mother. The struggle to differentiate herself and her own situation from these two identifications goes on for a very long time.

As could be expected, the neighbors are very threatening at this time. Her badness is shown up and they observe her mercilessly. During the first weeks of this violent release of her destructive fantasies, she again had implored me for some new drugs, for help to escape from this dreadful confrontation with herself. She even wanted to go to the hospital again, and my promise to receive her, if necessary, had to be kept up for a long time. But the alarm she feels cannot prevent her from glowing with bright colors as she witnesses the fire.

3 April 1966

Marion has been burning up her mother and Ellen for almost five weeks, and by now the storm has subsided a little. Marion reports happily that grandmother has returned again. She disappeared during the depression of September 1965 when Marion entered the world of entirely bad objects. She had appeared in glimpses since then but was lost again when the rage surged up.

Marion calms down at once and feels better when grandmother is near. Here she is seen on grandmother's lap (middle left), this group is surrounded by a golden light. It is again striking to observe how much this support from the internalized grandmother means to Marion. The capacity to love and feel loved is still inextricably connected with the image of grandmother. "I try to be like her. I quietly take Lillian in my lap, telling her tales." Periods of happy closeness to Lillian still become interrupted by hate and sudden urges to kill her. Marion in the summer camp with mother's letter in her hand is still crying (top).

The slowly developing revolt in her has made her put on a pair of high-heeled shoes in real life. She tells me that she has some still smarter ones at home, but does not dare to use them yet.

Grandmother's long absence indicates that even a firmly rooted, good, internalized object may disappear when rage and hate toward the primary object, the mother, prevails. Grandmother returns unaltered, however, as if she has been waiting for the affect storm to quieten down.

In the drawing the painful and humiliating childhood memory of the Easter holidays is still seen to burn up before the eyes of the crying Marion (bottom right).

140

7 April 1966

The bad objects of her childhood have to burn long and thoroughly in the flames (top). Their power becomes reduced, and with the support of grandmother (bottom) Marion is now able to face a later and very painful conflict with her mother, burdening her with a heavy guilt-feeling. Before this memory was actualized by becoming relived experience, she was again extremely anxious as so often happened when some stirring conflict area was being fended off. As described in her life story, as an 18-year-old she had left her mother after a quarrel with her, after having lived with her and Ellen for a year. During that year she had in vain tried to regain her earlier closeness to her mother. To leave meant giving up this hope, it was a renewed experience of loss. However, it had also been an aggressive act. Marion knew that her mother was ill and had needed her help. She now recalls how her mother looked small and poor, only pretending to be unaffected. Surely her mother was as unhappy as she herself. Marion sobs and tenderly pats the cover of the couch. She also vividly remembers how her own compulsive perfectionism developed after she left mother, together with her slimming, her fear of being fat, her loss of menstruation. The guilt lessens as her regret and sorrow are lived through. Also her compulsion to put everything in order diminishes. "Yesterday I let the mess Lillian made just lie about..."

Here she illustrates how she takes her bag and leaves, crying. The big doors seem to be irretrievably closed behind her. This is the central theme for the time being both of the drawings and of our sessions.

Below, Marion sits on her grandmother's lap.

142

143

10 April 1966

This time Marion is seen to return in order to repair the damage done to her mother and to work through her sorrow and guilt. She regrets that she didn't herself take the initiative to talk things over instead of leaving. After all, she was no child any more. "I haven't had a good day since then . . ." She recalls that the slimming had to do with an inner prohibition to eat, and that the enjoyment of food from then on had become barred to her. She had been chronically underweight ever since that time.

The warmth surrounding the group of grandmother and Marion (below) has a curious resemblance to the flames around mother and Ellen.

However, a new crisis is developing. In a week's time Marion will again be extremely disturbed, wanting ECT and hospitalization, even speaking of suicide. The material emerging from repression soon explains what it is all about. The heavy pressure on her by her internalized bad objects – symbolized by the firm grip of her two guardians – is beginning to lessen. Her revolt against her own submissiveness, already well under way, is now felt to threaten her marriage. The cry for more freedom, for being set free from her imprisonment, is suddenly experienced as a craving for sexual freedom too. As this revolt approaches consciousness, she begins to panic, feeling the whole security of her existence threatened. In some dramatic sessions she cries that she wants to remain a child. Then follows the rage toward her mother for locking her up, for punishing her, for thrashing her into obedience and submission. It was her mother who had sent her into her marriage just as she had sent her to the summer camp. She can't stand this prison any longer. There is also emerging an intense envy of her daughter for having a father, and she can report a dream where she enjoyed some sex play with a male doctor in the hospital. It is as if her oral fixation, her exclusive preoccupation with her mother, is beginning to loosen, giving way to the first stirring of her genital sexuality.

144

12 May 1966

While Marion struggles with the emerging threat of her developing genitality, more signs of the maturational process come to the fore "Marion-the-mother" is seen slowly to acquire the forceful colors of Marion between her two guardians; there is a slow gathering of her split self into one identity. The child on her lap is still unreal and in some drawings is left out altogether. It is the relationship between Marion and the bird – an aspect of her own mother – which now seems to be the important one.

Nuances are added to Marion's conceptions of her mother. She realizes her own demanding attitude, perceiving her own greed, calling herself a spoiled child who wanted everything – far more than her solitary mother was able to provide. She acknowledges that she herself has not been able to give Lillian the love she needed. By now she has worked through her jealousy of Lillian's therapist and becomes a loyal co-operator in her daughter's therapy. She has acquired the courage to buy herself some smart clothes and from time to time wears earclips. The long period of affecto-motor discharge has evidently effected an entire change in the use of her musculature. She reports that she is much stronger, even heavy housework doesn't tire her any more, causing no stiffness and aches.

Her genuinely increasing independence at first caused her severe anxiety as she imagined that this might eventuate in the loss of her husband. In her drawings he had appeared as a yellow supporter (drawing from 25 June 1965 onwards), not to be distinguished from her grandmother, to both of whom she had clung in fear. She now feels guilty because of her emerging wishes for wider sexual experience, she hasn't known any man other than her husband. She ventilates her protests against the confinement of marriage, and then, however, to her own and her husband's surprise she makes sexual advances towards him and discovers that she is again able to experience delight in sexual play. She had lost her pleasure in sex after the death of her mother, now six years ago.

26 May 1966

Also, she experiences all the more intensely her yearning for a father, and she revolts all the more against the grip on her by her mother and the therapist. In this drawing she introduces "a father", with herself sitting on his lap and Lillian standing at his side. As she never had a relation to a father figure, she explains that she has put him together from some aspects of her husband, of an uncle, and of a father of a girl friend at school. This father never acquires color in her drawings as he never was a real person, either in external or in internal reality. Marion says that nevertheless it is good for her to have him there, he reduces the power of her mother.

The struggle for independence causes Marion to draw herself with an arm raised (bottom). Until now her arms had been depicted as typically hanging down, passively held by the mother and the therapist.

The identity between the three Marions in this drawing is almost complete: "Marion-the-mother", Marion with the bag (middle), and Marion in the grip of her two guardians. On "father's" lap,
however, she appears as an orange shadowy being (top left). Mother and Ellen are still in the flames (middle left).

The incipient sexual life with her husband immediately reduces her jealousy of Lillian. She feels that she herself now has some satisfaction, she feels richer. Her bodily, libidinal hunger, so characteristic of the puerperal depression, slowly gives way to a feeling of saturation. It is as if her whole body – after having gone through the affecto-motor storms – begins to function in another way.

However, she is still essentially ego-weak. She has difficulties in structuralizing her emerging sexuality within the relationship to her husband. Promiscuous impulses and fantasies are breaking through, with an alarming intensity, giving me the impression that greed and hungry craving were transferred onto this new libidinal level. She has another motive now for staying indoors: her fear of her own erotic impulses. Till now her persecutory fear of the observing neighbors had been the prime cause for not going out.

148

2 June 1966

Marion's arms are no longer stiff and passive. Here she raises one arm in crying protest against her mother and lets go of her hand. The father is there to support the development of her independence (top left). Marion wants more freedom in life. The only internalized model she has of an independent woman is her mother. She indulges in fantasies about her mother's "free life", at this time believing her to have enjoyed an unlimited sex life with her male friends who took her out in the evenings. To Marion they were all her mother's lovers. She has no image of a father to go back to and revive when her genitality emerges. This, in fact, seems to cause her a lot of trouble. In identification with her mother she in her fantasy turns to "unknown men – a different one every night", feeling a desire to posses what her mother once had. As a child she had been very jealous of these unknown friends of her mother. At the same time, quite consciously she yearns for a father, a trusted, kind man with whom to feel secure. She misses her first therapist – "a man and a father".

Marion is still unable to be a mother, Lillian is unreal both on her lap and beside the fantasy father. What concerns Marion is her own development.

Parallel with the revolt, on another level, there is an ever deepening yearning for the good aspects of her mother. She feels a deep sadness, wanting to lay her head on mother's shoulder and cry, cry. She remembers cuddling and playing on mother's lap. Also her mother's face sometimes appears sad and tearful, and Marion hopes for the reconciliation, for the all-forgiving embrace to come. However, mother and Ellen are still in the flames. The bird sometimes loses the good radiating orange completely, as here. There is still a long way to go.

18 June 1966

Here the grip of both her two guardians is loosened, the crying Marion at last standing on her own feet; the balance seems to be a little precarious, however. The various aspects of Marion are gathered into one identity and they are all crying. The "father" whom she has created out of her need for him, in fact, means a great deal to her. She imagines herself on his lap, loved by a man in whom she has a full, childish trust; she participates in an idealized love relationship, free from conflicts. Even Lillian is placed near this father, but as usual, she is depicted as a shadow. Marion, in this maturational process, evidently has reached the age when the father is of great importance to the development of the little girl. Here Marion's own lap is empty. This is actually the last time her daughter is seen in the drawings; for the next 16 months Marion becomes exclusively occupied with the task of growing up herself. Lillian only returns when Marion has developed into a genuine mother and an adult woman, in an illustration of her happy and normal family life (12 October 1967).

It is still necessary to have the bad objects – her mother and Ellen in violet and green – isolated from the rest of the drawing by the wall of the flames (middle left). Their power is greatly reduced.

23 June 1966A

What had been suggested in the foregoing drawings here becomes a manifest reality. There is again a shift in inner dynamics. Marion's two stern guardians are gone, never to return. She stands unsupported on her own feet in direct confrontation with her mother. Only these two, the main characters of the drama, are left. Nobody else will be seen for the next three months, when Marion is again ready to introduce "the father".

On the drawing she appears in three different relationships with her mother, all of them reflecting a very real experience, which will be expressed and lived through in the therapy. On top Marion is the small one, punished and beaten up by her mother. Below they can match each other in size, struggling with each other, both with their tears streaming. Their rage and excitation radiate in lines from hands and feet.

To the right a big, crying Marion, with an expression of rage and protest, has turned against the bird itself, the still non-human symbol of the unforgivable mother. The bird has grown in size, it has a more central place in the picture, it seems to draw nearer. The whole flank facing Marion shimmers in the good yellow-orange color. Marion complains that mother is sometimes overwhelmingly close to her; she has a need to defend herself against this presence of her mother.

There was, at present, a great clinical improvement. The storms of her destructive rage had subsided, her bad objects, having burnt for three months in the fire, had lost much of their power. Her impulsive urges to harm Lillian had to a great extent faded away, reflected in the drawings as a disappearance of her need to be controlled. Her sexuality was in ascendance, giving her new hope and confidence. She was again able to leave her home without anxiety and allowed herself to dress up in gay clothes.

As her therapist, I felt relieved, since I had not always been sure of the final outcome of this difficult therapy. I thought that with this new independence and strength, with this ability to match her bad object, the main work might be done. The future therapy would perhaps have merely the character of a working through and a stabilization of what she had achieved until now.

11. New Beginning. 10 Drawings

23 June 1966B

She lays the other drawings of her last homework on the table. I'm taken by surprise at an unsuspected development. Hardly has Marion gained her new independence and strength when she adds a drawing of herself as a tiny infant lying at the breast of the mother-bird, in fact, incorporated in the bird's body. Again one of these mutations occurs where something entirely new manifests itself.

As I have mentioned, during the time of her actual therapy I neither had the time, nor the need to study her drawings. This may have been an advantage. With the few exceptions reported, when I intervened directly in the drawing process, they developed entirely on their own. Through them Marion revealed a process that can now be studied and discussed in the perspective of her later development, unknown at the time of the creation of her drawings. Today one can see that this bird had all the time represented an unintegrated part of Marion's relationship with her mother. Marion had always drawn as a non-human entity that which was unconscious and far from integration.

After the bad objects of the nine-year-old Marion have been thoroughly punished and destroyed — that is when her own furious rage with them has been abreacted — she is able to approach the bird itself, now revealing its secret: it is the early mother, the infant's "breast-mother" whose breast is now found or refound. The baby is black, indicating the sorrow that still prevails. As the course of her further therapy will reveal, the Marion who becomes capable of loving, is now reborn.

However, the drawings alone betrayed the novelty of the situation. Marion's initial remarks might have led me to believe that a relapse into her earlier fusion with and dependence upon her mother threatened her hard-won independence. My comments therefore might unawares have supported her own strong resistance against this developing situation, her own fear of it (top right).

In this retrospective study I feel this development to be the third, decisive, turning point of her therapy, the two earlier ones being the times of danger when she had to be rehospitalized. I wonder whether many therapies do not also tend to stop *here,* before this new situation has been given an opportunity to unfold. The "return of the good object" is after all, not too elaborately described in our specialist literature, in spite of the effort of writers like Balint, Winnicott, Guntrip and Kohut to draw attention to the necessity of "benign therapeutic regression" in certain cases.[1]

---

[1] See Kohut 1971 for the description of therapeutic regression in patients with narcissistic disorders, to which group Marion also belongs.

30 June 1966

The good yellow-orange color spreads over the whole area. The situation in the drawing is the same, only the protesting Marion already seen in the foregoing picture has grown bigger (right side). Marion states: "I'm so close to my mother now, it is both good and awful, rather overwhelming. I'm raging against this closeness, fearing it, resisting it ... Especially is it frightening to be at one with that part of my mother which was independent, going out enjoying herself with men ... the mother I hated ... But I have to take in the good with the bad!"

Marion in part feels fused with her mother, she seems to experience the return to an early symbiotic one-ness with her, having to "take in" all of her. She strongly opposes and fears this feeling of melting into her mother. However, it is only a part surrender. The independent Marion is seen to maintain herself; she doesn't lose herself in her mother as she did once during the puerperal depression. The struggle with mother goes on elsewhere in the drawing. Partly Marion is the inferior one, being beaten up and humiliated (top left); partly she does feel powerful enough to be in control of her mother, punishing and reproaching her (bottom left). A straight-forward illustration of an internal sado-masochistic relationship.

However, this is no uncomplicated situation. Marion says of the bird that her mother can never be entirely human, she has been too cruel to Marion.

It is worth mentioning that Marion in this phase never spoke of the breast, of the pleasure of sucking, of being fed or of mother's milk, that is, of oral experience in its restricted sense of being nourished at her mother's breast. What she described was a feeling of one-ness, of closeness and warmth, of being enveloped in a loving embrace.

At this point begins the correction of "the basic fault" (M. Balint 1968). Or, in the context of object-relations theory, this infant at the breast represents the deeply withdrawn, libidinal ego which can only come to the fore after the oral-sadistic ego has displayed its rage and reached its aim of destroying the bad objects (Guntrip 1968).

From now on Marion's deep libidinal hunger and emptiness – though already alleviated by her developing sexuality – will slowly be replaced by saturation and happiness. A refueling with libido seems to take place through this refinding of her symbiotic mother. Going back to an earlier stage of the therapy, e.g. to the drawing of 9 October 1965, one will see that this symbiotic relationship to come is here hinted at quite unconsciously, by the identity of the mother symbol with the muddled head of the subhuman figure.

159

3 July 1966

The bird has gone, the mother has come. A mother with a lap and with arms to hold her child. This new situation accentuates all earlier privation and frustration. Only black and violet are used for this group (top right).

Marion the infant has come of age. She is not drawn inside her mother's body any more, she is sitting on her mother's lap. "At first I couldn't draw her as a real mother – with arms to hold me ..." Marion will need 87 drawings and seven months to consolidate her position on her mother's lap, after her first appearance at mother's breast.

At this point I again ask Marion what the drawings mean to her. She answers: "They are a part of myself. I draw one every day. When it isn't done, something is lacking, something of myself ... Even if they are difficult to make, painful, sore ..."

In her daily life she has gained more freedom of movement. For the first time she enjoys the company of others. Sexually she is relaxed and has more feeling. She quarrels with her husband as her equal: "He wants it *his* way, I want it *my* way ..." Just as Marion and her mother now are equals in their mutual battle, they are both alternately the big one and the small one.

Marion's ambivalence follows her into this new stage of development. All in all, mother's punishing aspect diminishes. "She is much milder. Sometimes I see her stretching out her arms for me. But then *I* refuse ... I cannot forgive her yet ..." With Lillian there is the same ambivalence: periods of close, warm contact, still ruptured by negative feelings.

Marion time and again discovers that the observing neighbors leave her alone when she talks things through. When she herself becomes conscious of and admits to what is stirring within her, there is no reason to feel seen through and criticized.

9 July 1966

The warmth of mother increases as indicated by the good yellow color developing in the mother with the lap. The black child re-experiences the long, long time of yearning and rage when she was without mother. Now mother has come back to stay with her. There are elements of mourning for the lost years, there is an experience of tearful reconciliation. Marion is scared, it is all too real. A part of her violently resists giving in to these emotions (top right). The battle of ambivalence is still raging.

The concreteness of the relived emotional stage is almost unbelievable. There is no question of just remembering; Marion *is* the child, she *feels* her mother's arms around herself, feels the profound change that the security of mother's lap will cause to her whole life. In Marion's still vivid visualizations of her mother, the latter seems to have her own movements and intentions. I have later met with this concreteness in other regressing patients as well, at a certain stage in those – rather rare – therapies where the early conflicts of primary love and primary frustration-rage are really actualized and lived through. Sometimes the patient remains orientated towards her or his original mother, as here. The therapist's influence on the developing love relationship is an indirect one, being based on background trust which make the reliving possible. At other times it is the image of the therapist which is internalized as the new core of the self (see Kohut 1971) at times the original mother and the therapist alternate or are merged into one new, "good mother". It is often an extremely painful and long drawn out process, the patients feeling defenceless and utterly vulnerable, anticipating the original trauma to be repeated and disrupting the regrowth of this very core of their personality.

Marion now leaves town with her family for the summer vacation.

162

12 August 1966

She is back in town after the vacation, and we again start our therapy. She reports a dramatic recovery. She is surprised that she has regained her appetite, she has enjoyed food and put on some weight. However, of far more importance is the fact that she can't remember ever having had so much fun before. There was no longer any inferiority feeling, no anxiety and internal pressure. She felt just as good as everybody else, she felt an equal to others. She feels deeply relieved; with a grateful heart she has thanked God for this recovery. She is allowed to be happy.

Her husband, who comes with her for a joint session somewhat later, confirms these changes. They both speak of a miracle. They now enjoy a normal sexual relationship, and for the first time in her life Marion experiences orgasm. The access to the libidinal relationship with her mother clearly meant the removal of a basic blocking of her own libido.

On the drawing the black, sorrowful child on mother's lap has disappeared. This child has now acquired the colors of the other representations of Marion.

Mother, still in violet, is surrounded by an orange halo.

From now on dreams begin to play a major role in the sessions and in her further development. Till now she had hardly told of any dreams. The emerging dreams were at this time curiously simple and undisguised. They were wish-fulfilling in the sense that she dreamt of her past days, the love objects of her childhood entering the dream space, and she relived her happy life with them. Many dreams were just a recall of situations of former real life, which now had added to them a peaceful and rich atmosphere of human togetherness, of belonging, of friendliness. Above all, her grandmother and the other inhabitants of the great common household – her aunts and uncles – came to life again. These dreams seemed to consolidate her inner situation. Her mother, however, wasn't represented among this dream population of hers.

"Mother is so mild and understanding. It spreads to Lillian. But then I get angry with them again. It is still good to draw myself as the big one, with the right and the ability to express my feelings" (bottom left).

164

23 September 1966

During the first weeks after the vacation she reports a steady improvement. "I feel so secure on her lap, feeling her arms around me. Then I want to cry, and tell her that I've been afraid for such a long time ..." "I'm not so split any more, more a whole person in all situations. Nor is mother different persons to me, she too is more one whole person now ..." "Toward Lillian I'm just an ordinary mother, a normal one, for the first time. She is more a part of myself. I enjoy reading and singing to her. That is something quite new ..." "The difficulty was that I was afraid of becoming like that independent part of mother ... I don't feel like a good mother then ... It is difficult to be both at once: a good mother and an independent person...".

She continues drawing the same situation: here, however, she again introduces her fantasy "father". Like the last time he appeared, he can't get any color as he was never real. Marion says she needs him all the same. On top (left) she takes his hand, below (left) she sits on his knee. She still has to express her protest against her mother.

I again believe that the end of the therapy draws nearer, that this phase will develop into a steady growth and maturation, the main inner work having been done. Again I'm wrong, underrating the difficulties of an ego-weak person who probably has had a faulty development from her earliest years. She is still immature, she still has to struggle for her differentiation and integration, there are still crises to come. What is essential, however, is that the earlier symptoms never return, the fundamental improvement is never lost again. In fact, this emerging contact with a supporting mother seems to be a prerequisite for her transition from a psychotic to a neurotic structural organization. From now on there is no internalized, bad object, no revengeful, punishing, primitive mother that weighs her down.

The internal threat will in the future be experienced not as emanating from the internal bad mother, but mainly from her own unacceptable impulses and desires. We are able to observe how the early form of ego immaturity implying a psychotic core in herself, is replaced by a more mature ego, from now on able to develop in a relationship with a "good enough" mother (Winnicott 1975 [1949]).

166

15 October 1966

While the basic feeling of security stemming from this deep change in her early relationship with her mother is maintained, another set of symptoms are now developing. She has attacks of headache, she complains of pains all over her body, but especially in her arms and shoulders. A fear of cancer is connected with these aches, a fear that she too, like her mother, will get cancer and die. I had the definite impression that she now was repressing something, as yet unknown to her; during the next months this repression in part was undone, enabling the underlying impulses and ideas to be worked through. With the renewed introduction of a "father" there seems at this time of his appearance to develop a rudimental Oedipal situation. This drawing is, however, the only one where the child-Marion this time acquires colors as she sits on her "father's" knee or takes his hand. Her real experience with a father figure seems to have been too meager. However, she sets up an Oedipal triangle; she believes me to be having an affair with the male hospital doctor of whom she has had some sex dreams, and she feels jealous. This is no more than a passing idea. What really alarms her is the breaking through of strong promiscuous impulses. She had believed her mother to have "a new man every evening" – men Marion never got to know. She feels envious of her mother, wanting those men for herself, glorifying this "freedom" of her mother's. As she now feels strong and fearless, there was for some weeks a real danger that she would act upon these unrealistic expectations, trying to realize them. To prevent her from going out and picking up some stranger in the street, I let her during the sessions describe her anticipated adventures: how she met a man, went with him, slept with him, left him the next day for a new one, and so on. In the course of our little psychodramas, reality begins to dawn upon her; she states that a sexual life like that would leave her with feelings of emptiness and unworthiness, as no human relationship was involved. The danger of acting out passes; what remained was a revolt against her marriage in spite of the new happiness she experiences with her husband.

Her longing for a father accompanies this actual state of hers. On his lap she is seen crying. I wondered if this yearning for a father represented a need to anchor her awakening genitality – which was still immature and greedy – to a trusted father, giving her an alternative model of a sexual relationship to that which she had acquired during her childhood. The unknown "lovers of her mother" – who probably only existed in her fantasy – were in her mind somehow put together into a sort of desired, multiple "father" figures causing the Oedipal situation she now lives through to be very distorted.

5 November 1966

There is steady progress at the deeper level, while the newly emerging symptoms are manifesting themselves at a more superficial level. In October 1966 she again took a part-time job, in the same shop where the colleague resembling her sister had caused her to break down in February 1965. The colleague still worked in the shop, this time without affecting Marion. Marion lives in peace with her neighbors and is able to have friendly chats with them. A recurring theme is that mother now allows her to dress up as she likes. In November she got her first permanent wave since the age of 16. "Mother is more understanding now. She wants me to have fun."

Interesting was her information that she was able to read books again. She had been unable to concentrate and "take them in" for many years. Thus various signs of a maturational process are appearing; there clearly is a new orientation toward life.

The "father" returns from time to time in her drawings, among those which elaborate her typical situations with her mother. Here she illustrates the usefulness of a father (bottom). He takes care of her while mother is occupied with the younger sibling, both of them in all-bad colors (top left). It is a situation giving her some security, she is not left out.

The big, crying Marion, reacting in protest and excitement against the lap-child, reunited with its mother, is a typical feature of these drawings, reflecting the still existing split in herself.

170

171

3 December 1966

Surely, the profound changes are being stabilized all the time. Recovery from what may be called her "borderline symptoms" is a fact. The depressive inferiority feelings, the feelings of insufficiency and guilt, the oppressive persecutory fears — the prohibition of fun and pleasure – they have all gone, never to return. What remained for a long time was a slight tendency to project — she easily felt observed when some forbidden tendencies stirred in her, and she wasn't yet conscious of what they were about. This was no more than a slight uneasiness and never kept her indoors any longer. However, the developing headaches, hypochondria, and bodily pains became even more pronounced. Some dreams hinted at what she was warding off: she had dream pictures of a funeral, far away, and she was scared and uneasy about these dreams.

The one-ness with her mother, giving her a basic security and enabling her to be at times genuinely happy with her own child, also had another side. The mother with whom she was now reunited, embodied cancer, death, and a supposed promiscuity, Marion still has to handle these aspects of her "bad mother", and before her laid the task of differentiating herself from her mother, to obtain a true individuality.

At this time Marion thinks her newly won happiness is a miracle. "I am as though reborn." "I've become just an ordinary human being." She has started to write down her dreams, bringing them to the sessions. Most of her dreams continue to put things right; they fill in the empty spaces in herself with good situations of relatedness to her childhood objects. She has also begun to write poems and rhythmic prose, expressing her rich feeling of being alive. It is a new way of expressing herself, in due time it will replace her drawing.

This picture reflects the way she works through her past. The scene is from the former Easter holidays in the cottage with her mother and Ellen. This memory was once "burned up" because of the unhappiness and humiliation she had felt on that occasion. She now actively returns to the situation. In the drawing mother and Ellen are seen in their all-bad violet and green. The grey little person to the right of the snowman is herself, at that time feeling depressed and inferior. The big Marion of today (bottom) has acquired the right and the ability to express her emotions, and relives the situation, in a way correcting the past event.

12. Maturation. 28 Drawings

9 February 1967

Beneath Marion's elation there had accumulated an anxiety that all this was too good to be true. Thoughts of death are disturbing her; all this richness she has gained access to might come to an end; there is a possibility of again losing it all. The thought of death gives a new dimension of depth to her poetry; she writes about life's deep sorrow and happiness. She reports orgastic experience of hitherto unknown intensity.

However, fright is creeping into her mind, and here it appears for the first time expressed in a drawing. Marion (center) stands crying, a wave of depression – the threat of loss – is illustrated by the figure over her head. To the right her husband and child are leaving her. To the left her husband has found himself another woman. A separation anxiety has been actualized which in the weeks to come will crystallize into its various aspects.

For the first time the mature female body is seen in the drawings, with breasts and hips, reflecting her changing body image. This woman is in the arms of her husband. The accentuated breasts betray Marion's own interest in the female body, projected into her husband. I didn't mention this but waited for a later, natural unfolding of this theme. Her dreams of a funeral, still far away, do not disappear again, more details are added, and by and by it becomes evident that Marion fights against the memory of her mother's factual death. I guessed that she was defending herself against the painful mourning process, which she would have to face in the future as a relentless demand of reality. Marion is also afraid that she herself might die. Her associations make it quite clear that she feels herself to contain the deadly cancer of her mother. Yet all the time she is supported by the newly-won good, internal mother. The split mother image accompanies her onto this new level of functioning.

I wondered if this separation anxiety, among its other determinants, might also be an echo of a very early loss of bliss, when once the early libidinal relationship with her mother went to pieces. Maybe it was a reflection of the early loss of Marion's happiness in her mother's arms, maybe a deep memory trace of some disaster beyond conscious recall was actualized by her new happiness. However, more obvious reasons for her fears were soon to evolve.

2 March 1967

All three Marions cry in this drawing. She explains it to be a sort of mild sadness, after the long years of unhappiness. From now on the child on the lap disappears altogether. She has grown out of this stage. Marion will in future represent herself in two alternating ways: as a rather formless, big Marion like here and in between the mature female body will appear, the adult Marion. Also her ambivalence from now on will be represented in a different way. For many months the big Marion has been protesting against the child-mother group, thus illustrating the conflict in herself between the baby who needs and enjoys mother's lap and the other Marion who rejects this situation. The "father" who comes and goes in her drawings is also here seen for the last time. The maturational drive seems to bid her to give up the safety of being a child with a good father, and with access to her mother's lap. Marion tells me that she has dreamt of a naked man on whose lap she was sitting; she felt him to be a sort of father because she experienced such trust and security. "Maybe it's because I'm so happy with my husband." She still seems to be groping for the unique relationship with a good father in order to canalize her sexuality towards a secure and lasting relationship with one man. However, she is threatened by emerging sexual impulses that continue to embarrass her. She recalls her sexual play with a girl friend in school, she is surprised by an urge to masturbate, in dreams she has seen her mother naked. Her envy of her mother's "free life" is a constant threat to her actual happiness.

She now reports a steadily growing intimacy with her daughter, telling me of their joy of being together in play and cuddling. She has had some night dreams of having a second child. The better her relationship with the internalized mother of her own childhood, the better her relationship with her own child.

Now that the oppressive feeling of constantly being criticized and observed has disappeared, she also lets go of her compulsive perfectionism. She recalls how it had developed along with the slimming and loss of menstruation when she left mother at 18. She is now quite relaxed in this matter, and she is therefore less annoyed with her household duties.

30 March 1967A

A new group is added to the sorrowful theme of loss and separation. Up to the right Marion herself has found a new lover, she herself has a sexy, mature, female body. With this final admission of her wishes, she becomes able to talk more freely about them. It is now possible to straighten out a complex undercurrent of irrational thoughts.

Marion gives the impression of having reached the stage of an adolescent girl, expressing her hunger for expansion, for trying out new experiences. Above all, she complains that she missed out on the time of dating, on the time of having a free and changing choice of boyfriends, of playful erotic adventure. She never had a youth of this kind. She can't help rebelling against the chains of marriage, against her adult obligations, in spite of her happiness. There is no man outside her marriage in real life, however, to whom she feels attracted. Her further associations throw light on her fear of cancer and death. When mother divorced her husband, she could again have resumed her "free life" – so at least Marion believes. Instead she contracted cancer and died. Marion's own wishes to leave husband and child will inevitably lead to her own illness and death, as it happened to mother. The features of a hysteric neurosis become all the more evident.

These conflicts need many months of working through. Sometimes her difficulties, ambivalence, and bodily pains are so intense that she is angry with me for having made her more healthy. "It was easier to be ill. I felt nothing." Her dreams sometimes give her a hint of the nature of her present state. She has dreamt of a child with a very big stomach, a very greedy child, wanting everything.

In the funeral dreams she now has to confront the frightening sight of coffins. Marion is labile, angry, happy. "It's difficult to be alive."

178

30 March 1967B

Here Marion does away with her half-sister once and for all. Ellen is virtually thrown out of the picture. It is her last appearance in the drawings. The sibling is represented in her purely bad aspect, as indicated by the green color. It is in fact the rival who disappears. This is quite a different situation from the one, depicted in her drawings of August 1965, when the huge Ellen in mother's bad, violet colors threatened to destroy Marion's life. At present, Ellen's visits to town are no longer felt as a provocation against which defences have to be mobilized. They are friendly together; Marion's jealousy has faded away. From being the hated, newborn sister, the carrier of Marion's conflicts with her mother, Ellen has now been differentiated as a person in her own right — a definite achievement of Marion's maturation. In fact, Ellen in the drawings has been depicted in her own green color for more than a year, while earlier she always carried the violet of mother in addition to her own green. However, mother continues to be drawn in both violet and green. Her unfaithfulness and desertion are irretrievably mixed up with the birth of the half-sister.

Mourning in Ambivalence
19 Drawings

22 April 1967A

Marion works through her themes again and again in her drawings. She now has pains everywhere, and her hypochondria has brought her to two different medical specialists; she has difficulties in controlling her fear of cancer. She is upset, anxious, weeping. In dreams and day-time visualizations, elements of death and disease, a funeral and a coffin are pressing upon her. Mounting rage and despair at last bring forth this representation of herself. Marion-the-mourner, draped in the black veil of sorrow, suddenly enters the drawings, this time as an adult woman. Angry slang words from the streets of her childhood are written down in the upper right corner of the drawing. Once they represented the children's defiance and revolt against the grown-ups. Marion had been heavily punished by her mother for using such words. Here they return, surely vitalizing her verbal expressiveness: "Witch, shit, cunt, cock, old hag . . ."

It is the last and decisive mourning process of this therapy which is now in ascendance. Mother's factual death has to be faced. To realize the loss of the mother whom she regained internally only such a short time ago makes Marion wild with protest and despair. She draws a series of black mourners, resembling figures from an ancient tragedy in their fury and agony. To quieten herself down Marion has taken to drinking, bottle and glass are seen in the upper left corner.

As we are going to observe, her still intense ambivalence toward her mother makes this mourning process strikingly different from the one concerning her grandmother. That loss could be expressed by the symbol of the dead tree, serene and beautiful. This time the symbols will be of quite another character.

Through the struggle with this ambivalence, however, Marion will achieve a fundamental maturation. The mourning process itself mercilessly confronts her with her own hate and rejection of her mother barring her from the full internal possession of her love object. Intertwined with the motives of mourning there now in her drawings follows one situation after another of differentiation and integration, for us to witness through her own convincing illustrations.

22 April 1967B

More black and angry mourners. Tears are streaming from her eyes, angry, dirty words are streaming out of her mouth. She accepts that he has to face the terrible coffin with her mother's dead body inside. It appears to the left, Marion standing before it with her arms uplifted in a beseeching movement. Bottle and glass are seen (bottom left), Marion drinks. To the right, next to the terrifying mourner, is seen the small, abandoned and depressed Marion who appeared in her drawings a couple of months ago (9 February 1967). At the right edge of the paper her husband and child are seen leaving her. This theme of abandonment is gone from now on. A new and forceful Marion has appeared on the stage, able to express and take the responsibility for her conflicting emotions without separation anxiety.

27 April 1967A

Here she stands alone, face to face with death, the reality and presence of which force Marion into a passionate expressiveness which she has never had before. Her ambivalence is intensified and almost unbearable. On the couch she bangs on the walls, kicks, cries, shouts. Mother's presence is so vividly visualized that I almost see her myself. Mother is again seen as the skeleton, the ghost, who wanders about in search of her child. Or the weeping mother approaches Marion, seeking reconciliation, wanting to embrace her daughter. Marion's fright and anger flare up, she refuses to receive her mother. The ensuing experience of emptiness and a terrible void makes Marion cry for her mother to return. It is all vividly dramatized in our sessions. "When she approaches me, I turn her down. When she leaves me I stand hammering on the lid of the coffin to make her alive ..."

Now she is angry "as a tiger", now she is dissolved in tears. She feels a pressure inside, she has to contain all sorts of anxieties and emotions.

In the drawing Marion confronts the coffin. The mother, however, is still securely locked up and invisible.

27 April 1967B

Marion had taken in the whole of her mother, lying at her breast, and now struggles with the conflicting elements in herself, due to this internalization. It is indeed difficult to be at one with a mother who though loving and supporting also incorporates cancer and death, as well as – in Marion's imagination – representing a free life, unburdened by marriage and duties. In fact, it is too difficult. Another non-human symbol differentiates from Marion, a snake in mother's bad colors. It symbolizes something different from the earlier bird that changed into the mother with a lap and arms to hold her child. The snake – so Marion tells me – is the temptress who whispers to her about enjoyment, fun, sexual pleasures. It is the bad sexual mother who left Marion dressed up and went out with her admirers. "She let me stay with grandmother. She worked hard, but went out to enjoy herself whenever she wanted . . . I envy her. I feel the urge to do the same . . ." The snake is seen to leave Marion, turning its back upon her.

The visualization of this snake is quite concrete. Marion once saw it curl up on the radio at home, once it appeared on her lap. "As I know what it means I don't get scared." She is not very surprised, intellectual reflection isn't her strength. She seems to have kept a child's ability for imaginative thinking, in concrete pictures. This also explains the surprising capacity to draw her imagery. As one might expect, her urge and her capacity to draw subside as her maturation progresses. She hasn't the abilities of a real artist.

The mature female body appears here for the first time in colors (bottom left), reflecting Marion's deepening emotional involvement with her new body image.

Under bottle and glass (upper left corner) there appears household furniture, the symbols of her drinking and her dutiful slavery respectively. The despairing black mourner still occupies the center of the drawing.

189

5 May 1967

The new Marion, again in colors. Of this picture she says: "A new Marion develops, the old one (the grey little figure below) is swept away as a shadow — as if it were on wheels ..."

She tells me that she seems to have slept all her life till now. Her eyes are opened, she sees the world as it is, and she is often shocked and disappointed, struggling to understand all the intricacies of social life. She reacts with emotional outbursts, hurt and angry. People aren't kind, neither towards each other, nor toward her. Somehow she has come out of a shell, she is alive, finding the world strange and difficult.

Marion's lack of social experience begins to make itself felt. She has never really been present in the world, never fully experiencing it. She has been in an emotionally withdrawn state, compliant and subdued. Now she feels quite overwhelmed from time to time. "When I draw, I see myself better, more clearly ... I then get a better grasp on things, sorting them out in a way ..."

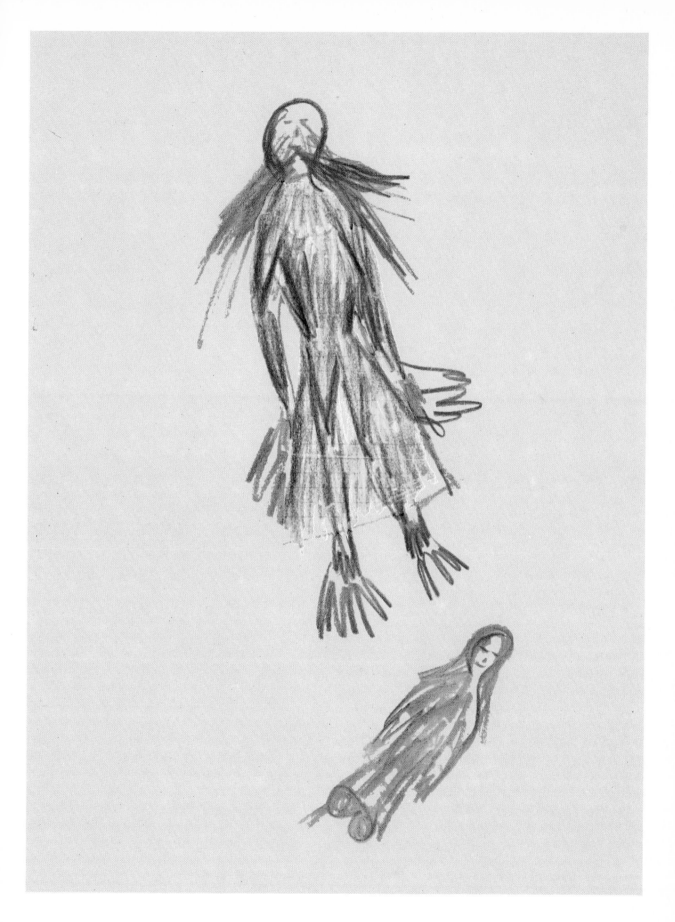

11 May 1967

The ordeal Marion is going through makes her at this time so impulsive that one might speak of a slight hypomanic swing of moods. She laughs and cries, hates and loves, her language and manners are uninhibited, she uses vulgar slang words. This phase of uninhibited expansion can be seen in other borderline patients too, when the almost lifelong pressure from the internal bad object is diminished. Or in other words, when the depression lifts, there follows a state of disorganization with its danger of acting out. Marion has all sorts of pains and somatic complaints, all sorts of feelings: "Everything rushes upon me ..."

In the drawing Marion is stripped of her protecting clothes, that is, they have become quite transparent. The inner excitement is symbolized by the lines radiating from her limbs. The snake has turned round and approaches Marion. "The snake is so close, nearly suffocating me ..." The snake tempts her, whispering about the free life. It also symbolizes the mother she rejects, whom it is so difficult to make really human. "When I'm most happy, my thoughts turn to mother ... Then I feel the pain and get scared, thinking of cancer and death. She died when she was about to have a good life ... I have a good life now ..."

"I'm so like her in many respects ... Now I'm sometimes just as angry as she could be."

It is a difficult task to differentiate herself from her mother and all the same hold on to the indispensable good internal object.

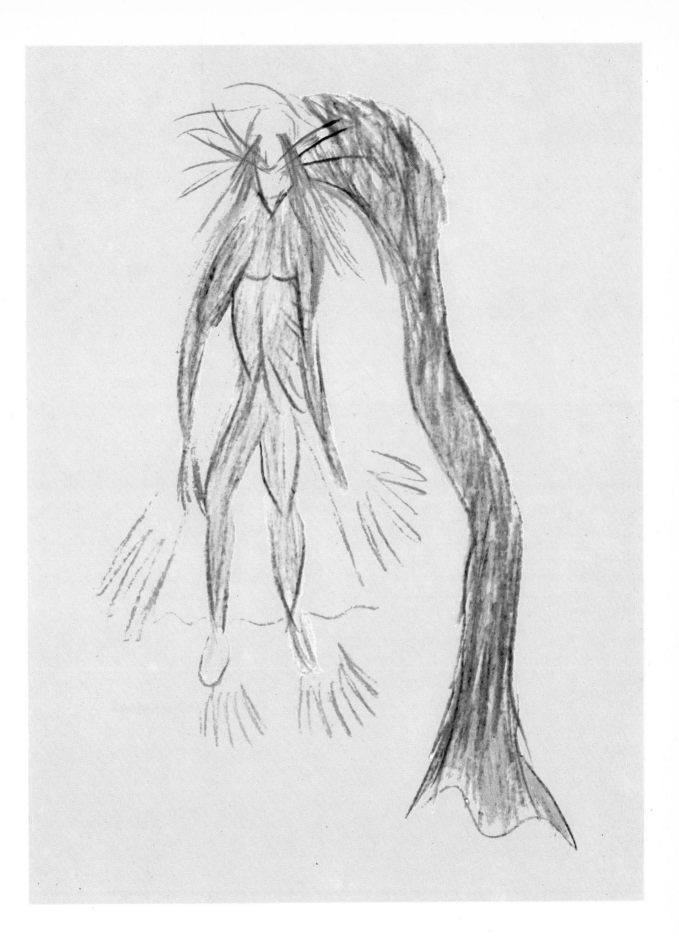

13 May 1967

A drawing where the various elements of her present themes appear together. The preoccupation with her mother's coffin and dead body continues and adds a macabre aspect to this mourning process. She tries in vain to defend herself against the emergence of these thoughts and visualizations. They flood her as obsessional ideas of decay, stench, putrefaction. She has to face them and deal with them. Hidden away in the corner (bottom right) wrapped in a cape, she is able to stand looking at the mother in the coffin, which has now opened up. "This is what is left of my mother. The worms are eating her up." An all-bad violet mother is seen, surrounded by all-bad violet worms, devouring her. Marion's all-bad, destructive, greedy possessiveness is projected into these worms. By repeatedly drawing this picture, Marion slowly becomes aware of the meaning of these obsessional ideas. In other, later drawings, the worms penetrate the walls of the coffin, while here they stop outside it. Later Marion also draws "her own fingers" instead of the worms. These ideas were extremely frightening and painful to work through.

The neighbors' houses with their windows again appear, the observing eyes mercilessly watching Marion's mad ideas. During this phase she felt spoken of as the woman who had been in a madhouse.

On the drawing, to the left, she draws herself big, strong, naked. Not even transparent clothes are left to her. She is crying and excited, the whispering snake has come quite close. She feels the snake to be digusting, far too near, somehow slippery. The fact of its being non-human indicates that Marion is repressing something in connection with her mother of which she is not aware.

The husband, somewhat shocked by his wife's impulsive behavior during the last weeks, now joins us in a session to unburden himself. However, he also states: "Marion is quite on top, self-assertive, gay, far more secure ..." She dresses up in bright colors, feeling that her mother wants her to do so. Ideas of having a second child occupy her mind more and more.

The curious little gray form, to the right of big Marion's feet, is "my regret for an aggressive remark I uttered ..."

16 May 1967

The coffin, the devouring worms, the snake are represented in a lot of drawings. The very mourning process borders on a pathological condition, were it not for the fact that it occurs as a phase in her therapy. Here appears a picture where there again occurs a sudden leap in functioning as a result of the acceptance of the greedy, possessive elements in herself – "the worms". Marion lays this drawing on the table with a happy and excited exclamation: "This is a *whole* human being. The snake is all inside myself, all the bad colors belong to myself. I've seen so much evil in other people . . . in fact, I'm not different myself." She has become able to contain the good and the bad inside herself, without dissociating the bad to the outside.

This step forward in integration is further reflected in Marion's comments: "It is as if I'm discovering the world around me – it all comes rushing upon me, sometimes it is too much. I wear dark sun glasses to moderate it a little ... My thoughts are coming, I am getting a broader view of things. I'm now able to do a lot of thinking ... I see so much wickedness but I realize that I'm like that myself . . ."

It is here tempting to quote Winnicott: ". . . (the patients) would like to be helped to achieve unit status, or a state of time-space integration in which there is one self containing everything instead of dissociated elements that exist in compartments or are scattered around and left lying about." (D. W. Winnicott (1971): Playing and Reality, p. 66).

Marion now realizes that her conflict between her responsibility toward her husband and child and her yearning for a free life is really inside herself and not primarily caused by the whispering voice of the snake.

20 June 1967

The struggle to keep this badness inside herself goes on for about 6 weeks. It is only with some difficulty she is able to bear it. To the upper drawing she remarks: "I'm feeling stronger every day now." Then the houses of the neighbors are small, she doesn't care what others might say about her.

However, the snake and the badness are liable to come out again, as ugly words and as anger (below). She gets scared, the neighboring houses become bigger. "Then I feel like a snake myself." She says that no one will ever be able to suppress her again, she fights every attempt by others to do so. In fact, she often misunderstands others and over-reacts, being suspicious of the neighbors, who might want to turn her down again. She speaks of her feelings of freedom and health, but she is often afraid of losing her friends because she so impulsively speaks up and fights back. She tells about fun, and about the richness of new ideas coming into her mind. She brings me her poetry, which is just as unsophisticated as her drawings, merely serving as her full personal expression of joy and sadness, life and death. Her new ability to think improves her handling of the household budget. She has had difficulties in planning her expenditure, often using too much, giving in to her impulse to buy what attracts her at the moment. This had been a point of marital conflict. She was very little concerned about money.

An outright feeling for justice is developing in her; she hates slander and refuses to take part in it. She protects the weak ones, and often becomes involved in disputes with the neighboring housewives. "I feel like the angel of justice."

12 July 1967

On the one hand there is Marion's joy in reporting about her progress. On the other hand there is something frightening, dark and shadowy, with which she still hasn't dealt sufficiently. Cancer, death, the obsessional ideas of stench and decay are still lurking. She is, in fact, in a rather chaotic state, with all sorts of impulses and feelings whirling about inside herself. She has so much to contain, sometimes she feels bursting with it all. All sorts of migrating pains, from her toes to her finger tips, bother her. She remarks that her muscles probably *have* to ache, she has been tightening them for years to suppress all her rage and despair: now they seem to be thawing out. She is beginning to understand that her fantasies of a "free", that is, a promiscuous life, really are an expression of her greed, of her wish to take possession of all that was supposed to belong to her mother's life.

The dawning of a new experience is here concretized in a picture for the first time: the symbiotic one-ness with the all-good mother, stripped of every trace of bad colors. Marion explains that she herself is both mother and child. The way they both feel is quite identical: there is a happy, sensual, close tenderness and togetherness. However, something interferes with this, something black and horrible (to the right), something like death and destruction.

Her conscious ambivalence toward mother is still intense and is enacted during the sessions. There is a to and fro of wishes for reconciliation, followed by urges for revengeful rejection; she wants to reach the loved one and to punish the frustrating one. Marion's agony affects all her mind, body and soul. She feels the outcome of her conflicts to be a question of love or destruction. The split in her is still a deep one, but now it seems to be polarized into the two clear-cut opposites of life and death.

At this time we again part for the summer vacation.

19 August 1967

There has again been a long summer break, during which Marion has drawn and struggled. When we again start our sessions, she is seen to approach the death of her mother in a far more composed way. Gone is the wild despair, gone are the devouring worms, the smell of the decaying body. Mother is seen peacefully lying on her death bed, flowers in hand. Above, the despairing Marion, of the time of her mother's real death, is standing in the window, having her last glimpse of her mother. At that time she had been quite unable to express her feelings.

Below the Marion of today recalls this sight and reacts with a full emotional outbreak of sadness and sorrow. There is a dancing rhythm in her expressive movements, which makes one think of a beseeching death dance.

Her migrating pains and hypochondria have again brought her to a medical specialist. Her fear of having cancer is a constant feature of this phase.

Her vulgar speech and uninhibited behavor had already quietened down before the summer vacation. In revolt against her mother's coercive behavior she had taken up into herself the naughty child she once was, with games and fun, in order to integrate this Marion in her total adult make-up.

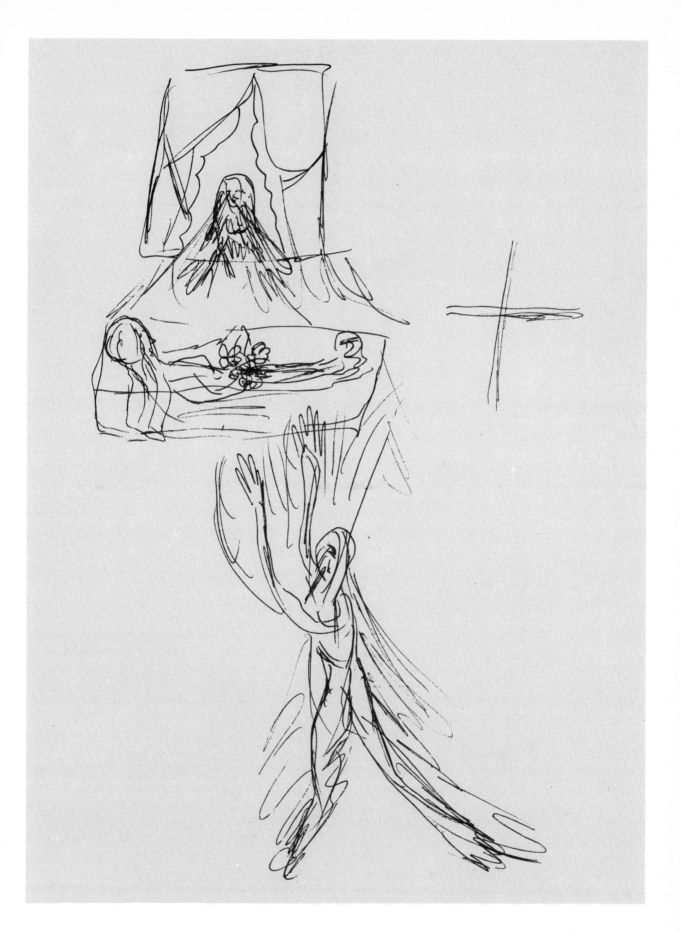

203

24 August 1967

A naked, excited, and crying Marion is standing alone in the midst of the neighbors. She says herself: "It is me, around me are the neighbors. It feels different now ... they don't disturb me and interfere with me any longer. I owe them nothing ... they are just Mr. this and Mrs. that. I have grown much stronger in this respect ... Curious, I wonder if they look at me in just the same way, only as Mrs. M. and that is all ... Before, I felt them looking straight through me, reading my thoughts ..."

She draws a big, unafraid Marion with the right and the ability to be just herself. The others may look if they want to, she has nothing to hide. A picture of self-representation, of revolt against her own former compliance and fears.

7 September 1967A

Again a drawing of mother on her death-bed, pale and grey. Marion herself is drawn in forceful colors displaying her intense emotions (middle right). The former Marion is seen in the window, paralyzed and expressionless (top). Under the death-bed Marion has drawn the "dead and empty ones", explaining that they belong to the underworld, the realm of the dead ones. Lately she has repeatedly dreamt of this underworld and its ghost population, having felt frightened and uneasy about these dreams. She links this underworld up with her dead mother as well as with her own former state of being dead and lifeless.

I'm again struck with the resemblance of Marion's spontaneously chosen themes to the structure of some ancient tragedy. Here the background chorus seems to appear, accompanying the passionate drama of mourning with their sad murmur of the inevitability of death.

7 September 1967B

The fusion with her mother, from which it is so difficult for her to differentiate herself, has many aspects. To this drawing Marion comments: "It is me and my husband in sexual intercourse. Mother is somehow *with* me in sexual matters (the green-violet part of the drawing). It is that strong sexual part of my mother which has now become a part of myself. Mother helps me, guides me . . . It feels so good. I enjoy sex very much these days." Her sexual mother, the very one she hated for abandoning her child to seek her own pleasure, is here accepted.

Marion has drawn herself in the good orange color. Her husband, like her fantasy father, will never acquire color (to the left). Is it because there is no early father image, once invested with the child's libidinal love, to transfer to her husband? Their relation is at this time a good and satisfying one. The urges for sexual adventures outside her marriage have to a great extent faded away.

7 September 1967C

But here the accepted identification and one-ness with her sexual mother is again dissolved. A green-violet mother representation is in part dissociated from Marion. Something is warded off, at once aquiring the non-human quality of the snake. Marion states: "When mother comes too close, I feel her to be sort of slippery. She becomes like a snake and I push her away. Mother wants to embrace me, she weeps and comes much too near ..."

Marion in yellow-orange is seen in the middle of the drawing, a full-breasted madonna-like woman. Her child stands beside her (to the right). A curved form, extending from the mother snake, is seen gently to stroke her face and breasts, betraying a yearning the nature of which Marion still can't accept.

Marion tells me that she feels shut in between the two obstacles appearing in the drawing. To the left is the ghost, the death and the emptiness, perhaps waiting for her in the future. To the right the snake prevents her from moving forward. It isn't yet quite clear what it is. "Something from the past concerning my mother and me ..."

210

14 September 1967

Marion here tries to draw the curious dream of the underworld which she has lately had again and again. She explains it to me: She enters through a sort of gate and goes downwards. Here she sees plenty of water, a great lake. Deeper down are the dead and empty ones, the skeletons (to the right). They also represent the sick ones, her fellow patients from the hospital. The therapist walks among them, helping and comforting them. Then Marion wants the therapist all for herself. The therapist is seen as a violet figure surrounded by a halo of yellow (bottom right). Marion herself is the gray figure in the middle of the drawing. Beneath her is the former mother-bird, in green and violet, all the pain from earlier times. From it radiate violet lines both toward Marion and the therapist, making the three of them into a single unity. To the left of the mother-bird another bird-like structure is seen, in yellow and red, also dragging Marion into the underworld (bottom left). "There is a force which is pulling me downward." The illness, connected with the therapist and the bad mother, is what she knows. Something in Marion wants to stay here, feeling attached to this world.

In the great lake situated above the underworld, naked women are seen bathing, caressing each other. Marion sees their big, soft breasts. Far away she sees "healthy youth", men and women, playing at the seashore, these women also with big, soft breasts. Marion explains that the dream tells her that it is possible for her to remain at each one of these levels. "But I want to get on to the healthy ones."

The dream seems to illustrate her own mid-way position between final health, a homosexual position, and her earlier attachment to her bad objects, to which also the therapist in part belongs. Marion, in fact, illustrates "the regressive pull", the fixation to the illness pattern which is a well-known feature of every deeper-going therapy.

28 September 1967A

Ever since the adult female body appeared in the drawings (drawing of 9 February 1967), reflecting Marion's development and changing body image, an undercurrent of homosexuality had been clearly discernible, while at the same time she developed and experienced a happy, heterosexual relation with her husband. However, when the predominantly oral fixation to her mother had lessened, the integration of her emerging genital sexuality had been no easy task. While her marriage slowly became meaningful and rich, there were at the same time these fantasies of a "free" life of promiscuity, in identification with her mother. They had now greatly subsided. At present another aspect of her sexuality emerges. In nightly dreams and in her fantasies of naked women, in memories of sex play with girl friends, her homosexual preoccupation was by and by reaching her awareness. After the drawing of the underworld we were able to talk this material through. Marion had become fully conscious of her yearning for the soft female body. It had become clear to her that the slippery snake, the repulsive aspect of her mother, represented her own warding off of this yearning. Marion had worked with this new insight, and to this session she brings with her three highly significant drawings, drawn in the order they are presented here.

In this one she fully acknowledges her longing for another woman. Two women in sexual play and intimacy are drawn. Marion is the smaller one. Through this acceptance the final distance to the tender, sensual aspects of her childhood relation to her mother is traversed.

28 September 1967B

To this drawing she comments: "After my unaware rejection of the bodily closeness to my mother was all cleared up – after I had accepted that the slippery feeling felt like the homosexuality I wanted to deny – I suddenly got the feeling that my mother wasn't gone – there was so much warmth around her in the coffin, as if she really weren't dead. I'm standing beside her full of sorrow ..."

In the drawing the greater half of her mother next to Marion is shining in the good colors of love. The other half remains in the darkness, where the evil green and violet are lurking.

The final splitting of the mother image into a good and a bad representation takes place before our eyes. Further events will prove that this time it is a successful split. Marion is from now on able to isolate this good part of her mother from the bad one, thus for the very first time creating an all-good internal mother whom she can love without interference from her ambivalence. The genuine libidinal tie to this good aspect of her mother is now restored in internal reality.

28 September 1967C

Here mother and child in golden colors are seen beaming with happiness at their reunion. Marion states that she herself is both the mother and the child, the experience of love is a shared one, felt similarly by both of them. In contrast to the drawing of 12 July, 10 weeks earlier, the happiness is now undisturbed by the ghost, by the fear of death and destruction. The split is completed. Marion is able to relate to the restored good aspect of her primal mother, the mother of symbiosis, with the full richness of primary love. To Marion it again appears as a miracle, just as when her grandmother returned as a loving internal support when the mourning process was lived through. It was the lack of this good mother deep down that had caused the puerperal depression with its appalling feelings of emptiness and emotional starvation and the concomitant impossibility of loving her child. The daily confrontation with this misery had left her no possibilities of escape. She was unable to identify with her mother's harsh ways of child-rearing as her grandmother had given her quite a different model of mothering. The vicissitude of her relationship with her internal mother (and grandmother) and its effect upon her attitude to her own child can be traced all through the treatment.

Marion now says: "Mother is so often a support, speaking to me like grandmother did before. It is new to me ... it has never been like this." And she also says: "Sometimes it is just like this now – such a good feeling between my mother and me – such a warmth. Sometimes it is difficult to accept – because of the anger ..."

Her drawing now by and by comes to an end, no new themes appear, only some working through of the earlier ones. The colors disappear. She remarks herself that she has got so many ways of expressing herself that drawing isn't necessary any more. The therapy from now on centers on a working through, on a support for her further stabilization and maturation.

5 October 1967

Only with the security of the restored, all-good mother inside herself is Marion able to return to the reality of her actual life in her drawings. The colors are gone. It is as if she were coming out into the bright daylight from her long, inward journey, which took her through all the terrors of the underworld.

Her love now flows freely from the internalized good mother to her husband and child, giving these relationships in external reality a new dimension of warmth. Here she illustrates her happy sexual life with her husband: "The warmth has come into this relation too – it is just like that warmth which now exists between my mother and me . . ."

The mutuality of a genital sexual relationship is depicted. The long battle with her internal mother had already given her the feeling of being her mother's equal in strength. As a result of this inner situation she now also feels an equal to her husband, the sexual relationship with him having for her lost its earlier, inherent meaning of her own inferiority, of her own slavery and imprisonment.

Marion has depicted genuine, happy motherhood as a state of shared happiness, in identification both with her own child and with the good and tender aspects of her own mother. Here she tells us that this state was experienced when, at the same time, the level of genital sexuality was reached. Both aspects of loving seem to be inherent in healthy femininity.

12 October 1967A

And here, from the depths of her grateful heart, comes this drawing. It depicts the way she conceives of her actual family life. "Never in my whole life have I been so happy . . ."

The drawing presents three independent people, united in a group, but each of them clearly an individual. Mother and child are in contact with each other. Age and sex, adult and child are adequately drawn. The tree and the mountains indicate Nature of which the group is a part. Compared with the drawing of e.g. 6 August 1965, the process of growth that has taken place between these two pictures becomes convincingly illustrated. In the former drawing Marion presented herself as a clinging, little girl of the same age as her 3-year-old daughter, seeking support from the threat emanating from the unintegrated part of herself – this threat at that time comprising the relationship of the furious bird (destructive impulse) with the bad object (Ellen in mother's violet colors).

The HERE AND NOW living has at last become a reality.

223

12 October 1967B

Confident in her own heterosexuality and her sexual relationship with her husband, Marion now gives free reins to her homosexual trend without warding it off any longer. This drawing illustrates a dream: a woman (identified as herself through her associations) is lying down while a lot of naked women approach her with their desired breasts and soft bodies. Later she tells of repeated nightly dreams in which she is in bed with a naked woman. For a long time she takes delight in these dreams, without guilt-feelings or anxiety, enjoying the warmth, softness, and smell of the female body. It is as if she can at last satisfy her pent-up yearning for her mother's body, once depicted in the early drawing of the despairing little girl standing outside mother's house without a door (drawing of 9 April 1965).

In real life there was no woman to whom she felt attracted in this way. It was all lived through in fantasies and dreams, and in the emotional transference relationship with her female therapist, who sometimes appeared in her dreams as one of the naked women.

I felt that this phase served the integration of an aspect of sensual love, representing an identification with and taking-in of femininity, being a full, deep saturation replacing her earlier feelings of emptiness in relation to her mother. It did not seem to disturb her heterosexual maturation and her happy relationship with her husband. On the contrary, I think it helped to stabilize her heterosexuality.

One might also understand this phase as the last extension of her desperate craving for her mother's body, which now had multiplied into a lot of desired women able to satisfy her yearning.

The homosexuality became gradually integrated and ceased to be an isolated feature of her sensuality.

19 October 1967A

The roots of this desire for the female body, which she now accepted so whole-heartedly, are here acknowledged by Marion. She recalls the frustrating situation when her intense longing for her mother's care became conscious: mother stands attending to the newborn Ellen. The desired breasts are drawn in their proper place. Marion in the foreground displays her intense affects at this sight.

We may infer that a too sudden, traumatic loss of these breasts through an insensitive weaning had been the primary cause for Marion's creation of the archaic, all-bad mother image. This loss could never be compensated, this mother image could never be resolved and integrated, because mother continually exposed Marion to separation traumas, and also because Marion's great fear of her unpredictable and temperamental mother prevented open and natural interaction with her.

The resort to the grandmother, who became the good object of Marion's childhood and saved her capacity for love relationships, had been Marion's way out of her conflicts with mother. For this very reason, however, she may have remained with her infantile conception of an all-good grandmother and an all-bad mother, shunning the elaboration of her mother image. The psychic reality and vitality of this mother image has been demonstrated in this report, as has been the possibility of changing its impact on the personality through inner work in a therapy. In her treatment Marion had to confront belatedly her relationship with the internalized mother, and this proved to be the essence of her own maturation.

227

19 October 1967B

This hard-won restoration of the loving and beloved aspects of her mother will be of far-reaching consequence to Marion. At present, however, this love accentuates her grief at the factual death of her mother. She has gathered all her good memories of their relationship, and the bereavement she now feels deepens the ongoing mourning process. The irretrievable loss has to be lived through and accepted. Here Marion illustrates this last farewell.

The dual aspect of mourning has again been concretely depicted and is similar to the process she illustrated when mourning her grandmother. On the one side the intense agony of facing the loss – the real farewell. In the case of her mother's death Marion also demonstrates that mourning implies the working through and resolution of the mourner's own ambivalence. On the other side the final, spontaneous instalment in internal reality of the love object, with the return and preservation of the earlier love relationship – an unforeseen event conceived of as a miracle. For Marion, the blocking of the mourning processes had left her with an unbearable feeling of emptiness and depersonalization.

A fundamental process has come to an end. The good internal mother will never again disappear; she will remain the foundation deep down of Marion's health, around which in future she will organize her further maturation. This is the definite achievement of her long treatment.

However, the observer may perhaps already have asked: how did Marion dispose of the other side of the split mother image, that green-violet, shadowy part of the mother seen to recede in the picture of 28 September 1967, where the definite, successful splitting is illustrated?

We know that Marion's drawings always reflect a psychic reality. Thus some problems must have remained. In fact, the ambivalence had been too deep and pervasive for the bad to be simply assimilated by the good. It will later become evident that an internal, bad mother had been successfully repressed and displaced for many years, made possible by Marion's acquired ego-strength and at this time with neurotic defence mechanisms at her disposal. However, a later crisis will bring "the return of the bad object" (Fairbairn 1968).

13. Report December 1977

Will a therapy like this prevent another period of disturbance? How stable is her health?

Ten years have elapsed since the therapy proper came to an end. I have been in contact with her during all this time and have followed her further development.

During 1968 and the following years – in gradually spaced-out sessions – there was a stabilizing of what she had achieved during her therapy. The HERE AND NOW living had its problems. First of all, she needed some sort of after-education. The long period of compliant living, the lack of true self-expression, seemed to have prevented a natural maturation of social skills. She had not been able to gather and integrate sufficient experience of how to interact with others. The new Marion's encounter with the world around her often caused her disappointments and surprises. She had to discover that her own standards of truth and values, developed during her therapy, were not at all shared by everybody else, as she had been at first inclined to believe. She often misjudged the reactions of others, sometimes interpreting them as wilful malice. She had to be taught to discriminate between different social situations, some of which required only conventional politeness, whereas others implied a real possibility for initiating more intimate relationships. The new Marion, with her warm, uncomplicated trustfulness, at first thought everyone to be like herself. She was in some respects like a child, and her difficulty in putting herself in the other person's place caused her many bitter disappointments. She was labile these first years and needed the support she got from me.

As time went by I could notice an ever-growing identification with the internalized, loved mother. This mother was at first conceived of as another person than Marion herself, talking to her and guiding her, living a sort of life of her own. Marion reported that she was becoming more and more like her good mother, and she was proud of it. The very best of her mother's character traits were gathered into this internal mother, now constituting Marion's ideal self. "Mother never tolerated any injustice, she always defended the weak ones. So do I." "Mother could be as angry as a tiger. So can I – sometimes I'm frightened by my own violent anger ..." "Mother was an independent woman, she just didn't put up with everything. Nor do I." Marion lived out these qualities freely and consistently in her actual relationships. She also reported that her looks resembled her mother's more and more. Everybody said so.

She continued to be a housewife, with occasional jobs as a shop assistant. Some plans for further education were abandoned when her second child, the daughter Myrna, was born in 1970. This time she experienced a rich, warm mothering with all the happiness of sensuous bodily closeness that she had missed the first time. She took steps to prevent Lillian from suffering in her eventual jealousy reactions to the baby and sent her to her former child therapist for some support. The therapist found Lillian's development satisfying. Marion herself took care that Lillian freely expressed her feelings about the rival sibling. There were no difficulties of importance. Marion now had to choose between her mother's and her grandmother's way of upbringing. After some doubt – her husband was in favour of more discipline – she wholeheartedly decided on grandmother's model. With genuine understanding she cared for her child's autonomous growth, at her own pace, granting her the right and the time to live out her actual level of development without too many and too strict demands for obedience and nice behavior. To some extent she took over the therapist's handling of the child in herself, during the storms of her therapy. Sometimes she really fought "like a tiger" against the more conventional standards of the people around her, as she had now become unafraid of openly expressing her anger toward those she was fond of.

When she came to see me, she often brought with her letters, a sort of free-associative diary, including drawings of herself. Without exceptions these drawings were of an adult woman, filling out the whole center of the paper, and with her angry reaction to some actual stress situation expressed by radiating lines from her mouth, hands and feet. There was never any use of color.

Thus no great change had occurred in her actual living conditions, only the quality of her life and relationships was profoundly altered. She felt content to be "a whole human being", life had become intensely real to her.

There remained one area of conflict, however, which she was not able to solve. These conflicts contributed to a new wave of symptoms in 1975, which illuminated the way in which she had unconsciously disposed of the negative aspects of her mother during all these years of satisfactory health and happiness. This conflict area comprised her relationship with her mother-in-law.

As already mentioned, Marion experienced her mother-in-law's critical attitude as a serious threat and never learned to build up in herself a reasonable defence against her disapproval. The mother-in-law frowned upon Marion's permissive attitude toward Myrna, every time causing an upsurge of rage and tears in Marion. After her recovery, Marion openly revolted against her mother-in-law's very real domination of their family life and succeeded in spacing out the mutual visits and holiday obligations. I could point out to her that she invariably attempted to make her mother-in-law into a good mother, reacting again and again with violent disappointment when no change occurred. Marion's husband found himself in a difficult loyalty conflict and was often accused by his wife of not defending her and not taking her side in some conflict situation. During these years they both sometimes came to see me for a joint discussion of this difficult subject. At last they found – at least from an outsider's point of view – a socially acceptable though more distant way of relating to the husband's parents. I tried to help Marion to accept her mother-in-law as she really was, telling her that many families had to find a way of coping with a difficult member. The husband freely admitted that his mother caused them problems.

Marion felt supported by her internal mother in this conflict. Mother told her not to comply with unreasonable criticism, but to defend herself and speak up. So she did, to the point of scandalous scenes in the eyes of her strict mother-in-law, being determined not to let anyone subdue her any more.

On the other hand, she was deeply fond of her father-in-law. By this quiet, warm man she felt fully accepted and loved, just the way she was. He was now the only one to whom she had an unambivalent love relation. She also considered him to be her most important bulwark against her intruding mother-in-law, suspecting her husband to be too compliant toward his dominating mother.

Thus there was some resemblance between Marion's relationship to her in-laws and that of her childhood relationship to her own mother and grandmother. She never felt good enough for the former, never accepted unconditionally in her own right. In the latter she found full, loving recognition.

Even if the real characters of her in-laws justified her reactions, her vulnerability and violent disappointments pointed to some displacement of her original emotional ties. Till now this had been impossible to uncover; the irrationality of her attitude was hidden behind her rational and justified reactions.

There was also another, if slight, sign of unresolved conflicts. Whenever Marion for some actual reason felt down, she very often complained of pains somewhere in her body, probably muscular sensations. She then voiced a fear of having cancer "like my mother". This was never more than a fleeting, quickly passing idea. I considered it to be an inevitable result of the identification process with her mother.

Mourning in Panic

During the early spring of 1974 her father-in-law fell ill, and after some months of anxious uncertainty it became evident that he had an incurable disease and was going to die.

Again Marion had to live through a process of grief and mourning, this time with the full force of her emotional vitality. Her reactions were indeed formidable. The pain was unbearable for her, and she expressed her rage, protest, sorrow, and despair quite uninhibitedly. Her husband found it so difficult to understand and cope with her extreme reactions that both of them came for a series of joint sessions during spring 1974. This time a male psychologist joined us to support the husband, who already knew this therapist from the time of Lillian's treatment. Marion openly expressed her violent protest against the fact that the loved one was to die while the difficult one remained alive. She refused to accept that her father-in-law was to leave her. Some practical problems were also worked through, all of them centering around Marion's anxiety at not being able to keep the necessary distance to her mother-in-law, after the death of her father-in-law. We understood her reactions as an expression of extreme grief – with fits of uncontrollable rage, crying spells, throwing crockery about the house, too much drinking, even impulses to throw herself out of the car in movement. The couple needed support for several months. Her father-in-law died in the fall of 1974. For months afterwards there were long periods of apathy and lack of interest in her surroundings. Surely she was involved in a profound and protracted mourning process, this time again of a character different from that of the three previous ones.

Return of the Bad Object

Then, during spring 1975, some undercurrents of another sort of disturbance began to make themselves felt. She spoke more frequently of her fear of having cancer. The spouses had for a long time had some plans of moving. This move now became urgent for Marion; she couldn't stand her old home any longer. She pressed her husband for a solution without much regard for his very real difficulties in arranging this. He managed to find a pretty new apartment on the fourth floor, in a suburban area. Just before moving in, Marion became upset and tearful about leaving the well-known surroundings of her old home. I had seen her from time to time after the marriage therapy of spring 1974, and I thought her to be still vulnerable to every sort of separation. In a joint session with the spouses we talked the matter through. They settled in their new home in early September 1975.

Marion now became extremely restless, strolling about outdoors with little Myrna. Her alarmed husband noted some curiously inadequate reactions toward their new neighbors. Some were scolded, with others she was uncritically openhearted. Then a phobia of height suddenly emerged of which none of us had heard before. Marion maintained that she had always suffered from this phobia, only it hadn't been activated until they now lived on the fourth floor. She developed such a fear that for some time she was unable to stay alone indoors. She was so disturbed and desperate that hospitalization was again discussed. I no longer worked at the hospital, and this settled the matter for her. She wanted to be treated by me, and she found a solution herself. A girl friend, with whom she had been on good terms for years, had a roomy house. Marion took Myrna with her and settled down with her friend for some time, while Lillian stayed with her father. The friend lived on the groundfloor, and Marion calmed down.

In September 1975 we again started a psychotherapy with sessions twice – later once – a week. In February 1976 this treatment came to an end, replaced by infrequent visits by both spouses up to this day.

She was at once able to associate to her height phobia. A childhood memory stood at its center. She had as a little pre-school girl played as usual in the street, when her mother had arrived and heard her use some curse words. Mother, in a violent fit of temper, had thrashed her and locked her up in the bedroom. In panic Marion had jumped out of the window to seek refuge with her grandmother, who often acted as a shield against the temperamental mother. Marion now for the first time remembered a lot of unpleasant things about her mother, from the time before her mother's second marriage, that is, from the very time that she had idealized in the first version of her story. She now also clearly remembered that mother had not always lived continually with her in the old house before she was nine. Mother had from time to time found herself some other living place "high up on the floors". Marion also remembered how she had disliked visiting her mother in these places. She had to leave her games in the streets, had to dress up nicely, and always felt coerced by her mother's critical and impatient demands for good and obedient behavior. So the phobia was clearly connected with her mother's frustrating attitude.

After some sessions a deeper disturbance evolved. Marion again hallucinated the presence of her all-bad mother, and this filled her with headless anxiety. She was afraid she might jump out of the window to escape this dreadful mother, as she had done on that special occasion in her childhood. She also felt her mother to be so envious of her new, nice flat that she might push Marion out of the window. Only now Marion didn't live on the groundfloor and was afraid she might be killed by the jump.

Again she was in a state bearing some resemblance to her former puerperal depression. The "return of the bad object" had occurred, leaving little doubt that it was somehow the consequence of the death of her father-in-law. In losing his support, Marion consciously felt that she had been left undefended at the mercy of her mother-in-law. His leaving her, however, had also activated the dread of the primary dangerous object, the bad mother, who had unconsciously been identified with her mother-in-law. Surely her violent rage at being abandoned by her father-in-law, her most-needed love object, was also an echo of her former frustration rage at being left by her mother. Thus Marion was no longer able to repress this nuclear bad object, now activated by her own frustration rage.

Initially this rage was again experienced in a psychotic way, as a turning against herself of the bad internal mother's anger, reflecting the typical structure of an archaic internalized bad relationship: the internal object's retaliating attacks are the first derivatives of one's own repressed, unconscious aggressivity perceived consciously.

When these connections were cleared up, the psychotic quality of Marion's disturbance disappeared, and after three weeks with her friend she returned home. The rage and resentment toward her mother, unconsciously displaced onto her mother-in-law, were now becoming conscious and were worked through in the ongoing therapy.

A New Period of Drawing (525 drawings, 6 selected)

Even earlier, during spring 1975, Marion had brought her drawings to her infrequent talks with me, but she had never had the need to present them during the session itself. Now they were not felt as supplementing her verbal communication, for nothing proved to be beyond words any more. She seemed to be needing the aid of her own pictures to express herself and to clear up something which was alarming her. She handed me the drawings as she left, so that they were never integrated in our verbal contact. I had a look at them after the sessions and found that they served the concretization of the conflict area and the release of her emotions,

without much development of her themes, however. All the same, they had again been drawn specifically for me and shown to nobody else. Along with her drawings she also brought her free-associative letters, often with some written remarks and outbursts around a picture. Our contact had now become so sporadic that it never seemed natural to speak of her drawings, except by way of some cursory remarks.

This way of handling her drawings continued on the whole during the fall of 1975, when she was again in regular therapy, though she now from time to time explained what the drawings represented.

The latter drawings are not in the same class as the former ones, which possessed a highly dynamic power of promoting the integrative process by reflecting the ongoing, preconscious changes in herself. Their great number – 525 in all – makes it possible this time to compare her rather few themes – repeated again and again till she felt finished with them – with each other by their very number, which will be given in brackets behind each theme. This drawing period stretches all in all over an interval of nine months, between May 1975 and January 1976, but is clearly divided into two different periods of four months each, before and after the psychotic disturbance in September. During the three weeks when she had to take refuge with her friend, there were no drawings. In both periods of four months each, her respective themes were intertwined all the time.

During the first interval of May–August 1975, the return of her bad mother is only suggested by symbols, while Marion consciously elaborates her grief. During the second interval of October 1975–January 1976 only her childhood objects are on the stage.

May–August 1975

During this interval four themes appear

2 July 1975   *Sorrow* (48)
These drawings speak for themselves. They express the depths of sorrow at the loss of a love relation. The curved lines reflect the full swing of Marion's emotions, and the whole picture conveys profound tranquillity and majesty face to face with the inevitable fact of death. A sorrow beyond words.

These drawings are all of the same kind; they are all drawn in black crayon. The symbol of death, the coffin with the cross, appears 41 times beside the mourning woman.

A picture of herself as a mother with her two children on her lap (17) is not presented here. It is small and conveys the impression that Marion counteracts her grief by reminding herself of the riches she possesses in spite of all. This mother smiles conspicuously in May; in July she has begun to cry. In August this theme has disappeared.

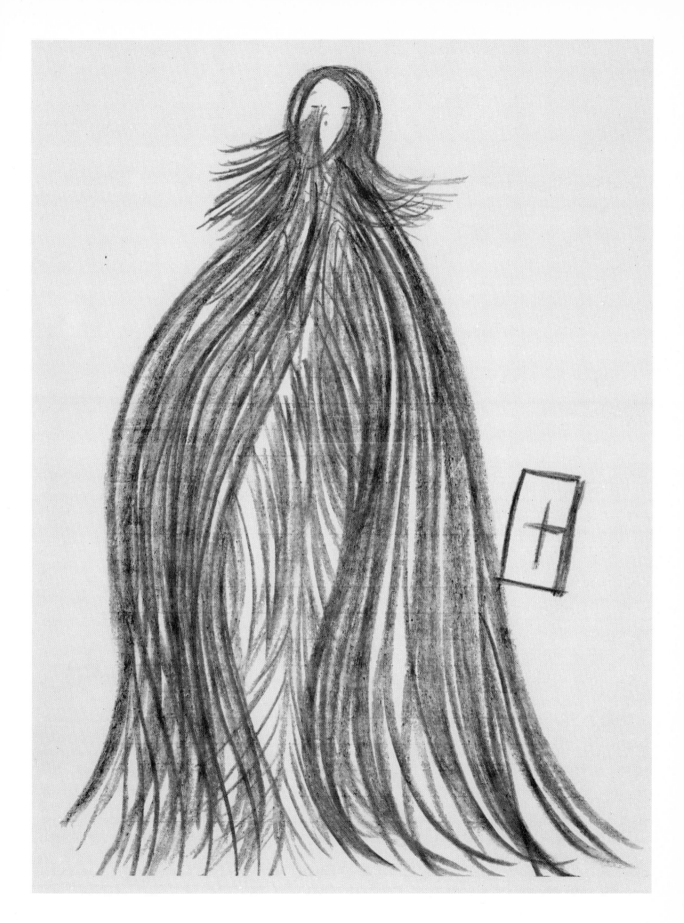

10 July 1975

The return of the bad object (41) are the only drawings in which she approximates her former style of using her color scheme. There are 28 of them that are quite identical with the one presented here. A slight variation occurs in eight of the additional drawings of this theme in the form of an orange figure that is drawn beside the bird instead of its orange duplicate. In addition, there are five drawings in only black or blue color, showing a small figure with some undefined masses hanging above it.

When these pictures appeared in between the other ones, their importance as a warning signal escaped me, as I was far from suspecting another return of her bad mother. Being quite unaware of it herself and by again just drawing "how it felt", she depicted something which had disappeared long ago and had again returned: the compact, all-bad mother-bird, which had once symbolized the area of psychotic disturbance in herself. But something is different now. Here one sees a duplicate of the bird (to the right) in the good orange color of love, disclosing that the good mother exists along with the bad one, even though for the moment she has retreated into the background. Marion at this time had no overt symptoms, although I had noticed some increase in her fear of cancer and also this compelling urge to move as soon as possible. There was some undefined, deep-seated alarm, the nature of which was in fact heralded by this picture. The representation of both the bad and the good mother is here in symbols, denoting that Marion is not conscious of their meaning.

This surprising drawing cannot but deepen our conviction of the reliability of Marion's unaware projection of her preconscious knowledge. The split mother image in her all-good and her all-bad aspects, still not unified into one whole mother, here appears before our eyes. This orange bird – which must represent the golden mother of symbiotic oneness whom she had retrieved in her earlier therapy – discloses the great resources now existing in Marion. The breakdown about to come, her miniature psychosis, was so easily turned into a fully conscious, renewed battle with her internal mother that one may feel confident that the hard-won results from her first therapy really were at her disposal.

236

18 July 1975

Protest and rage (38) concern her being abandoned by her father-in-law, and the coffin with the cross appears eight times. All the drawings are identical, all are drawn in black crayon.

This is another aspect of her grief, which had found such an uninhibited outlet in her impulsive, unpredictable behavior during spring 1974. She had virtually gone berserk from time to time. She was in a rage against fate, against the beloved one for abandoning her by dying, against all and everybody.

During the marriage therapy of spring 1974 neither she nor I could yet know that there had lurked an unconscious panic behind the intensity of her grief reactions, a panic at the prospect of losing the support of her father-in-law against the now emerging bad, terrifying mother. Not till this last therapy was finished, did I fully realize that the first therapy owed its good result to a successful splitting of the mother image, giving Marion an all-good, internal mother to relate to in trust and love, whilst enabling her to repress and displace the bad one. However, the bad mother had all the time made herself felt in Marion's fear of cancer — of being destroyed from within — and in her intense vulnerability in regard to her mother-in-law. Going through my notes of early 1968 this now appears quite evident. In the session of 1 March 1968 she had, for example, reported violent crying spells during the preceding two days. She had so intensely felt the loving presence of her mother, both of her mother of early childhood and of her mother after Ellen's birth; they had now fused into *one* good mother. For the first time she had felt that her hatred against her mother had totally vanished. The rest of that session, however, had been filled with indignant accusations against her mother-in-law, who was robbing Marion of the right to be herself, to have her own feelings, and to speak up without being rejected.

September 1975–January 1976

In this interval too there are only four themes. She has now changed to water colors and has abandoned her color scheme. Only her childhood objects are now on the stage. A great amount of rage and bitterness toward her mother had remained in Marion after her first therapy of 1965–67. Her renewed treatment soon became centered on her struggle to achieve autonomy, on her revolt against being controlled and interfered with by her mother, and on her great fear of mother's anger. Marion's remarks about the renewed appearance of the figure of PROTEST AND RAGE (84) – this time painted in contours of water colors (not presented here) – revealed that she now experienced her mother's strictness from the point of view of an adolescent girl, who had been forbidden to go out with boys, to smoke and drink, to dress up smartly, and to try out all the attractive activities of this age. In January 1976 there appear "boys" in these drawings, representing her adolescent sexual revolt against her mother's prohibitions. The therapist was drawn into Marion's angry rebellion, since the accusations through the transference reactions were directed against her.

All this happened only in her internal world; her actual behavior was not influenced by these conflicts. The primitive affecto-motor discharge reactions, once such a typical feature of her first therapy, were this time totally absent; Marion expressed herself through adequate verbalization.

It seemed to be necessary for her to integrate her adolescent revolt with the relationship to her primary love object, both to preserve the roots and the continuity of her own libidinal attachment and to safeguard her own autonomous adulthood through open self-expression. As in every successful adolescent struggle with the figures of authority, Marion too in the end achieves a reconciliation with her parent figures, at a new level of maturation (drawings of 1 January and 16 January 1976). Observations tell us that during adolescence again an object loss may take place, in part due to the failure of the adolescent's struggle, in part due to the fact that this phase demands a maturation of the parents too, who have to go through an experience of mourning the loss of their child as their own possession. It seemed to be of no significance for Marion that her mother had been dead for 15 years. The mother image was irretrievably connected with Marion's struggle for autonomy and with her most vital emotions of love and rage. Internal reality is of a timeless quality.

Conflicts with Mother (214)

18 October 1975

A. Sprawling on mother's lap
This is the one of her two themes, elaborating her relationship with her mother. Here she again sits on her mother's lap, where we left her in the fall of 1967. In comparison with the golden picture of symbiotic togetherness of 28 September 1967, she is here no longer content with her blissful, passive existence on mother's lap. She is sprawling in protest, waving her arms and legs, and so she does in all the drawings of this theme. She explains that mother holds her too tightly; she can't move or breathe freely. The drawings betray her renewed regression to childhood experience, but she has evidently matured beyond symbiosis and wants to "practice" her incipient independence (Mahler 1968). However, the drawings also reflect the unification of the holding, supporting, qualities of her mother along with the frustrating ones. Mother has a lap and two arms to hold her angry child, and we know from her first therapy how Marion struggled to be able to reach this lap at all. It is after all a very different experience to be angry with a mother on whose lap one sits, in comparison with having lost the mother entirely. The good mother, once retrieved, isn't lost in spite of this new wave of rage and protest. The bad mother is integrated with the good one, this picture being a further elaboration of the foregoing drawing of the all-bad mother-bird separated from the all-good orange one in the background. As Marion had no difficulties in mothering her second child (in 1970), these remaining conflicts of the time "after symbiosis" hadn't affected either her ability or her quality of mothering.

1 January 1976

B. The protective shield of her mother

Marion seems to sum up her actual position with the aid of two greatly simplified schemata, stating her internal relationship with her mother and her grandmother. She explains: "Both of them are standing behind me now, as a part of myself. I feel protected by them. But mother doesn't leave me space enough to feel really free, she squeezes and controls me". Marion's own text reads as follows: "Mother who squeezes me and wants me to be obedient".

This is again a combination of the good and the bad in her relationship with her mother. In comparison with the pictures of Marion with her grandmother, however, one sees how narrow is this space that her mother leaves her, giving Marion a feeling of being narrow herself. The outlines of her mother's body in many drawings impinge on Marion, illustrating the coercion that Marion still feels inside herself, as some sort of psychic scar.

This crisis, in fact, facilitated a considerable maturation in Marion. For the first time she was able to unite the all-good and the all-bad aspects of her mother into *one* mother, toward whom she felt a realistic ambivalence. She now clearly realized that she had identified her mother-in-law with the frustrating aspects of her own mother; that is she now understood that she had reacted identically to both of them, with rage, fear, and a feeling of being invaded and destroyed. After her first therapy her mother had been split into two aspects, so widely apart from each other, that mother's good and loving aspects were conceived of as protecting her from the bad and coercing ones. No wonder that she was never able to be at peace with her mother-in-law. A mother-in-law is very well suited for this sort of unconscious projection of the bad aspects of one's own mother, in order to make it possible to preserve the precious good aspects relatively undisturbed. Jokes about bad mother-in-laws are, after all, a source of great satisfaction.

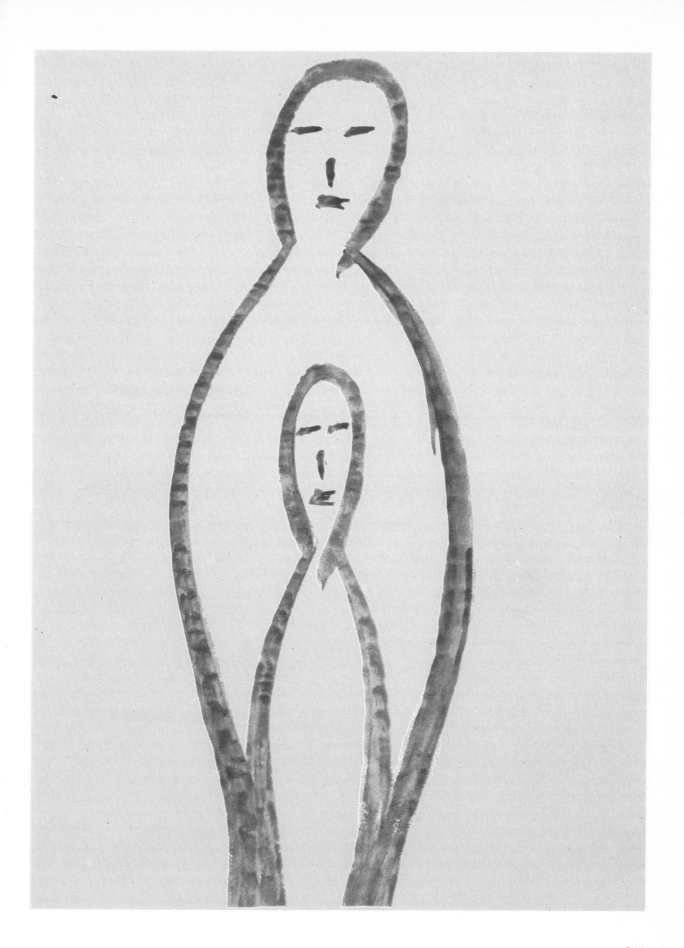

16 January 1976

The protective shield of her grandmother (83)

In these drawings one sees how grandmother, like her mother, is around her as a support. But here Marion has plenty of space. She stands up as a fully independent human being; in no drawing is she touched by grandmother. Here there is no impingement. Marion herself expands and states that she is able to breathe freely. Her written comments, accompanying the drawings, are consistently positive, in line with her expression of gratitude and love in the sessions. Her own text: "Grandmother and me".

And her comments: "It is so good to be with her. She allowed me to grow as I was, she loved me as I was. There is space enough to be just myself. I feel so quiet, so secure with her. She protected me against my mother's anger ..."

In all these drawings of the protective shields furnished by mother and grandmother the narrowness and spaciousness are consistently repeated and do not change. The difference is an established fact.

Marion had been brought up by "two mothers" — both her real mother and her grandmother — and she has told us about the difference in their handling of herself. She has given us her own experience of how children need to be treated. Her drawings reflect, however, the decisive difference between these two relationships. Through the time of early nursing the infant symbiotically fuses with an archaic image of its mother, split in undifferentiated clusters of "good" and "bad", and the differentiation of their further relationship occurs out of this early matrix. In this case the mother continued to be around, though not consistently taking care of Marion; thus she lost her mother, through frustrations, as her natural partner in the endeavor of growing up and was at the same time unable to let her go. The frustration inherent in this situation continued to impinge on Marion.

Through her last drawings we observe that at that time there existed two different kinds of internalized relationships in Marion; both are conscious, however. These two main childhood objects in fact constitute her "superegos", as she conceived of them up to the time of drawing. One gives support suffused with coercive control, the other is entirely approving and supporting. Maybe there are still more conflicts to be actualized in the future, as the picture of the mother relationship betrays still existing tensions in Marion. The process of coming to terms with her mother image will probably continue throughout life.

247

It may be of interest to compare the actual drawings of the impinging mother with some earlier drawing, e.g. that of 13 May 1965. In this early picture she also feels squeezed and impinged upon, but by some external, persecutory power, "the neighbors", depicted as nonpersonal black and red stripes in connection with mother's bad colors. The drawing betrays the paranoid elaboration of the nuclear conflict by an as yet undifferentiated Marion.

These two final, sober, motives of herself (the ego) under the protection of her internalized objects (the superego) should also be compared with, for example, the early drawing of 7 March 1965. Here one sees the greatly distorted, non-human and threatening mother image capturing a confused child – in fact a depiction of a psychotic internal constellation. In between the former and the latter drawing lies the whole therapy in which individuation has taken place, Marion's erstwhile persecutors now being identified as the impinging and pain-causing aspects of her mother.

The mourning of her father-in-law had led up to a confrontation with the still unresolved conflicts with her internalized mother. Her symptoms then – after the actual mourning process had subsided – can be conceived of as a progressive breakdown of her defences against the emerging, bad mother. At first there was an exaggeration of the already existing cancer phobia which had now become more understandable. Then came the urge to move, which Marion now understood as her wish for escape from the still unknown threat. Upon this followed the height phobia and lastly the mother herself, causing a miniature psychosis, which this time was easily overcome through the rather brief therapy. In fact, the good, external object – the father-in-law – proved to have functioned as a shield against the repressed, bad object. One may speculate whether some of those patients who display similar symptoms after the death of a significant love object in fact unconsciously feel threatened by the same internal disaster, though they succeed in keeping the internalized bad relationship itself repressed. It was again due to the weakness of Marion's defences that the mother image finally emerged, giving us the explanation of the dynamics at work.

The pressing character of Marion's childhood conflicts compared with her actual loss can be inferred from the drawings.

Drawings preoccupied with the death of her father-in-law, SORROW 48 and PROTEST AND RAGE 38, in all 86, should be compared with those depicting the old conflicts, RETURN OF THE BAD OBJECT 41, CONFLICTS WITH MOTHER 214, PROTEST AND RAGE concerning the revolt against mother 84, in all 339. When the support of grandmother, 83, is added to these, we are confronted with the fact that the actual loss is represented 86 times, the emergence of her internalized objects 422 times.

The father-in-law himself, whom she loved so deeply and who had achieved the status of her grandmother in her mind, does not appear in the drawings. We may conclude that he doesn't belong to the same deep level of her internal world as do her earliest objects, that is he isn't to the same extent an integral part of her own self. The outcome of the mourning related to her mother and her grandmother, as we learned from her first therapy, is of a far more pervasive kind.

The end of this last mourning process is that she forgives her father-in-law that he left her, and remembers him as a kind man she once loved and now misses. However, she feels his support. After the crisis of September 1975 she reported that he had "told" her to have confidence in herself, to go on rebuilding her own life. "He is quite near." *His* love, too, had become accessible to her by a process of internalization.

Marion and her family at present live a normal life. She has taken half a year of additional schooling and has a satisfying half-day job. She has been somewhat vulnerable to the separations inherent in normal life. Her second child has become a big schoolgirl, Lillian is a teenager, both of them developing toward more independence of their mother. This has caused Marion some minor, though rather painful, mourning, which she has had a tendency to act out as temperamental discontent in daily life. One may ask if she perhaps in this respect has become rather like her own mother.

The spouses visit me a few times a year, to report on themselves and to discuss some actual stress situation. On the last occasion (December 1977) the husband told me that Marion had changed very much during the last year, being now able to work through and discuss some passing conflicts in a far more composed and mature way.

They agreed that their relationship was an ever deepening one, to the mutual satisfaction of both partners.

Part III Discussion of the Material

14. Discussion of the Material

"... so many things that in the neuroses have to be laboriously fetched up from the depths are found in the psychoses on the surface visible to every eye" (Freud, S. *St. Ed.* XX, p. 60).

Perusing this book, the reader will probably have gained an impression of the remarkable richness in informative details given by Marion as she unawares depicted the therapeutic process. I have commented upon all her drawings and now I intend to discuss this material briefly from a theoretical point of view, placing it within the context of psychoanalytical theory. This may fail to interest some readers who may then cease reading at this point. Students of psychology and other professionals may, however, profit from this concrete pictorial representation of abstract conceptions which are often difficult for inexperienced beginners to grasp and to apply to their own immediate and intuitive perception of psychological processes.

Marion had suffered a psychotic breakdown at the birth of her first child, touching a deep core of disturbance in herself related to an archaic mother image. Since this breakdown disclosed her basic conflicts, sweeping away the elaborate psychic defences which usually complicate the clinical picture, her drawings have become uniquely illustrative of this treatment. Marion had the very special ability to concentrate on grasping and drawing the essentials of her preconscious imagery, representing at any given time the deep truth of her actual state of mind. In her pictures she created a sort of duplicate world of her daily existence, in part even of her sessions. Since she herself reduced the actual complexity of her treatment mainly to her confrontation with her mother images, we may assume that the ongoing differentiation of this relationship also reflects real changes in herself. Thus the basic structure of the process of change in this psychotherapy has become visible to the extent of being rendered almost transparent. Curiously her own account has acquired the features of a fable:

In an underground journey the bold heroine faces the monsters and the witch, dangers and sufferings, till in the end she reaches the goal of her struggle, the golden object of primary love. She becomes able to "live happily ever after" in the sense that she now can transfer her restored ability to love to her real objects of the outer world.

One might write a textbook of psychodynamics based on Marion's own version of the treatment process. Above all, the phenomenon of internalized object relations as dynamic structures can here be convincingly demonstrated. Marion simply drew her dead mother and grandmother as if they were still alive, and their power over her for better or for worse was tremendous. Thus she genuinely depicted the impact of "internal objects" in psychic reality.

On the other hand, Marion illustrates what can already be found in psychoanalytical literature in one perspective or another. So many interrelated issues are raised in this material that one has to turn to the relevant literature for a study in depth of the subject matter. However, therapists will in these drawings recognize the features of their own therapies. The depth and many dimensions of these pictures will make the visually minded observers feel a confirmation of their own life experience, as the material touches upon the very essentials of existence, genuinely reflecting general maturational levels and trends. A report like this also lends itself excellently to be worked over by others who may apply their own experience and theory to this evolving drama.

However, it is beyond the scope of this presentation to enter deeply into theory. I will limit myself to briefly outlining a perspective, open to corrections and amplifications, through which these drawings seem to fall into place, thereby drawing upon existing psychoanalytical research evidence — selecting, however, only a few representatives among the many distinguished workers in the field. My remarks must be thought of as a mere causerie for the sake of encouraging an imaginative understanding of psychodynamics.

I will here give a brief survey of psychotic puerperal depression, the very illness which brought Marion to the psychiatric ward. After a fragmentary excursion into present day developmental child psychology I shall point out some general features of the therapeutic process.

It becomes evident at once, however, that such a nonverbal raw material, when conceptualized and abstracted, can fit into different frames of reference. The process of integration is here observed to be a dialectic one, a forward movement through polarization of opposites, through reunion of splits followed by renewed splitting at higher level, and characterized by sudden, unforeseen leaps in the observable constellations. Those leaps are not analyzable, probably reflecting gradual, preconscious changes in her self-awareness, which in due time will be observable as a sudden change of structure in her drawings. They always occur after some challenge necessitating intense inner work. It follows that every logical and coherent presentation will invariably miss out on some aspects of psychic reality, as many writers on these topics may have discovered. Because of the inaccuracy of my own statements I have many times to refer back to the drawings, the ingenuity of which will provide the best understanding of the dynamics involved.

15. Psychotic Puerperal Depression

"Pregnancy is a crisis that affects all expectant mothers, no matter what their state of psychic health" (Bibring, G. 1961, p. 25).

Marion's drawings reflect the psychic structure of a woman who had suffered a psychotic puerperal depression. When her daughter was born, no good fairy appeared at her child's cradle. It was the bad one who emerged, the witch threatening Marion with eternal disaster. Marion's pictures tell us that it is the infant's mother who sees this fairy; she represents the powerful, evolving image of the woman's own mother, either in her all-good or her all-bad aspect. Marion's situation is typical for puerperal psychosis. The complete prohibition of libidinal gratification is the central issue, experienced as operating through the rejective, menacing mother image.

The profound hormonal and biological changes of pregnancy imply characteristic psychological changes. The healthy pregnant woman's attention will gradually turn inward; a spontaneous shift in her libidinal investments will occur, reactivating the mnemonic traces of her own infancy when in her mother's arms. Essentially governed by hormonal influences she will be prepared for the coming identification with her child, for the tender intimate relationship called the time of mother-child symbiosis in as much as both partners seem to belong to one unity. Under happy internal and external circumstances this stage will be enjoyed by mother and child in full mutual gratification of libidinal needs, as a basic, sensuous, undifferentiated experience of human closeness and security out of which a differentiation of their relationship will occur (Benedek, T. 1949, Mahler, M. 1968).

The woman's access to a good, nurturing mother image of her own is in health a natural consequence of these internal changes. To be able to mother her child she needs some amount of good mothering herself, eventually becoming greatly dependent upon her partner's capability for nurturing care (Lomas 1959).

Winnicott (1956) has observed the drive quality of early nursing, stating that the healthy woman seems to be possessed during the first weeks following parturition. In his own words: "This organized state (that would be an illness were it not for the fact of the pregnancy) could be compared with a withdrawn state, or a dissociated state, or a fugue, or even a disturbance at a deeper level such as a schizoid episode in which some aspect of the personality takes over temporarily". He observed that mothers recovered from this state a few weeks after parturition, and that this "disturbance" made them just the right kind of mothers. It implied a heightened sensitivity to the child's needs, protecting the baby with loving care against strong outer and inner stimuli. In his opinion, this beginning lays the very foundation for the child's psychic health and the further satisfying relationship with its mother.

However, uncomplicated devotion and happiness is indeed a rare state. The spontaneous activation of early libidinal experience triggers off the conflicts associated with the mother image. It is well documented that pregnancy tends to bring about a dissolution of psychic defences, with the inevitable emergence of unresolved conflicts pressing for a new solution.

The woman needs time to integrate her new state with her old self, if adaptation to the future tasks of life is to be achieved (Bibring 1959). The father-to-be goes through a similar, adaptive, process; in both partners parenthood is a developmental phase (Benedek 1959). Thus there will be a broad spectrum of possible individual post-partum reactions, from blissful happiness, via slight anxiety and depression, to more severe states of upheaval needing time to be worked through.

At the other end of the spectrum lies the psychotic puerperal depression, once more a state in which the woman seems to be possessed. Again some aspect of her personality takes over, this time, however, not governed by devotional care for her child. Marion's own account reveals that primitive rage and an enormous ambivalence towards her own mother is at the heart of the disturbance, barring access to the good mother image. The feeling of loss and the desperate hunger for libidinal gratification is an appalling feature of the illness, making it impossible for the mother to enclose her child in a love relationship. She is obsessed with the urge to destroy it, though she might wish to love it and be a good mother (Rheingold 1964).

In descriptive psychiatry the condition has been differentiated as a definite illness entity from manic-depressive illness, from schizophrenia, and from the more common states of anxiety and depression after childbirth (Hemphill 1952). The clinical picture, as described by others, seems to be quite analogous to Marion's case, with only some slight surface variations. Typically the disturbance is an unsuspected one. There is no conscious rejection of the child; the women have made preparations for it in the normal way. In contrast to the inner work done by more normal mothers, this area of actualized conflict has not been worked through. The disturbance therefore remains repressed, silent, covered by the psychic defences until it breaks through. Some of these women are possessed by a murderous rage and must be prevented from killing themselves or the child. In others a paralyzing depression dominates, accompanied by suicidal impulses. Guilt, conviction of her own insufficiency, persecutory and depressive fears mounting to panic accompany this basic disturbance in relation to the own mother image and the child. The clinical manifestation of hallucinosis is more or less pronounced.

The premorbid, overt character traits of these women will vary according to the defences set up against the basic fault. They are described as dependent, obsessional, and rigid (Hemphill 1952), as typically dominating their husbands (Lomas 1959), as extremely compliant with their own mothers (G. Douglas 1963). Marion's compliance and lack of self-assertion were a conspicuous feature of her personality.

For a deeper understanding of the disease I will here select a psychological investigation by Sylvia Markham (1961). Using a test battery she examined the ego structure and dynamics of 11 hospitalized women suffering a puerperal depression, comparing the evidence with that of a control group of non-psychotic women after childbirth. In both groups she found a reactivation of conflicts that had their genesis in early childhood, so this was of no special importance. What was of definite pathological consequence, however, and only found in the ill women, was the manifestation of a primitive symbiotic attachment to their own mothers, fraught with massive hostility and intense dependency needs. These women had failed to develop self-identity and unconsciously still felt enclosed within the mother's ego structure. From this vice of ambivalent symbiotic relationship, escape was. almost impossible. These mothers had no access to good memories of their own infancy and could not transfer patterns of genuine motherliness to their children. Due to their regression to a disturbed symbiotic stage, they were now unable to differentiate between their mother, their own self, and their child, and the destructivity of their own frustration rage was directly transferred to their child.

There was a marked difference in ego strength in the two groups. The women in the control group were able to cope with their depression, using defensive and sublimatory devices, and they could transfer libido easily from their own mothers to their children.

This report, in addition to Marion's own account, establishes the fact that a maturational arrest has occurred in at least a certain group of puerperal psychotic women, to be discussed in the next chapter. However, the deep core of developmental failure remains probably repressed in many cases. At the time of childbirth the woman's access to a supporting relationship, an internal or actual one, in which she herself can feel contained, is essential for her ability to transfer libido to her child. To some extent a good, real relationship can compensate for her failing access to the internal, good mother image. Pregnant women, feeling somehow threatened by an unknown disaster, are sometimes observed to "adopt" a substitute mother for the time of childbirth and early nursing.

Marion herself was depleted of internal resources at the time of her pregnancy. Firstly, no father figure had ever canalized her attachment away from her exclusive dependence upon her mother figures. Secondly, she had not yet recovered her good grandmother, dead a year before her child was born, as a reliable internal support through the process of mourning. Marion's relation to her dead mother was suffused with problems, by far exceeding her capacity to solve them, no access to the good mother image being possible. Due to the lack of differentiation in herself, her husband at that time seemed fused with her two bad objects: her mother and her mother-in-law. The latter was perceived as being just as rejective as her mother. Thus all her conflicts were unresolved. Nothing warned her against mothering a child in this state of confusion. For the first three months after delivery she tried to resort to mechanical nursing, feeling nothing. The child, however, became an inescapable menace to her flight mechanisms, and the illness erupted through her defences.

Puerperal psychosis is also known to occur, not at the birth of the first child, but manifesting itself at some later childbirth. This again brings up the question of internal or external support against the reactivation of the dangerous core conflict. Though the woman has been able to identify with her first-born, some later child may represent a hated rival sibling causing the destructive hate to surge in her. Some essential, protecting love relationship may in the meantime also have been lost, disturbing the delicate balance of inner forces. Thus we observe the protective function of Marion's father-in-law. His

death — occurring seven years after her satisfactory recovery — causes a return of the repressed "bad mother". In her case, however, the renewed struggle with this all-bad mother image now occurs at a higher level of integration, as can be seen in the drawings, where the all-good mother image has remained an internal possession deep down. Marion's happy natural mothering of her second child, born in 1970 after the decisive therapy of 1965—67, serves to demonstrate the effect on nursing of this access to the loving and beloved mother image. The remaining bitter conflicts with her mother had not affected her relationship with this child, the drawings revealing that these conflicts belonged to the time "after symbiosis".

Marion spontaneously depicts genuine, happy motherhood as a state of shared happiness, in identification both with her own child and with the good and tender aspects of her own mother. It is a libidinal love experience, for which the woman is prepared during pregnancy, through the libidinization of her own early infant-mother relationship, dependent, however, upon the quality of her own symbiotic stage with her mother.

Yet, we remain with the problems of the split mother image. The good and the bad mother image may obviously both exist as definite psychic realities in the same personality.

16. The Split Mother Image

"... the less predictably reliable or the more intrusive the love object's emotional attitude in the outside world has been, the greater the extent to which the object *remains* or *becomes* an unassimilated foreign body – a 'bad' introject in the intrapsychic emotional economy" (Mahler, Pine and Bergman 1975, p. 117).

Psychoanalytical knowledge makes us realize that Marion's experience of her mother's relentless persecution of all expansion and joy certainly didn't correspond to her mother's actual intentions. The image of the witch will be the legacy of the very young child's primitive hate and fear of the frustrating aspects of its mother, and the powerful impact of this image indicates an arrest in Marion's own maturation.

One must assume that Marion's mother considered her child in good hands with its grandmother, and that no choice remained for her but to resume her own life. The way we see their relationship through Marion's eyes indicates mutual frustration and disappointment. Marion's rage stemmed from her deprivation of a continuous relationship with her mother, to whom she was deeply libidinally attached, probably from the very time of breast-feeding, and also from her feeling of not being accepted in her own right. Her own hostile rejection of her mother is typical of the angry child who in this way deepens the chasm in the continuity of its mother-relationship. Typical also is the child's savage need to punish its mother for her unfaithfulness.

Psychoanalytical development psychology, based on observations and psychotherapies of young children, has greatly contributed to the understanding of the psychic structures underlying borderline and psychotic conditions in adults. This is a vast topic and not even the scantiest outline can be given here. Only some few facts of the research evidence relevant for this material will be reported.

We owe to Melanie Klein, among her other contributions, the clinical description of "internal objects" which she observed operating in her child patients. The child externalized these images onto toy figures in play therapy; in this respect Marion's drawings are analogous to child play. Above all, Klein acquainted us with the "good" and the "bad" mother concept, the highly subjective, internalized, split aspects of the real mother, created by the little child's own, undiluted, rage and love reactions. Klein described how actively the child elaborates these images in an ongoing process of projecting them back onto the mother, then again to internalize a mother image, "colored" by its own emotions. Those images, often greatly different from the real mother, become intensely real to the child, since they are connected with very real emotional states of pain and need tensions, on the one hand, and states of relaxed happiness, on the other. The splitting processes are regarded as inherent in psychic life: "It is splitting which allows the ego to emerge out of chaos and to order its experiences. This ordering of experience which occurs with the process of splitting into a good and a bad object, however excessive and extreme it may be to begin with, nevertheless orders the universe of the child's emotional and sensory impressions and is a precondition of later integration" (Hanna Segal 1973).

While Klein stresses the child's own distortions of reality, Margaret S. Mahler (1968, 1975) completes this perspective by underlining the child's dependence upon the character of its real relationship with its mother. Mahler's research mainly covers the preoedipal phase, the first three years of life during which the rapidly developing child needs very real support and encouragement by its parents, especially by the mother, as its emotional development seems to be bound to the object of its primary love, the mothering person. Mahler's emphasis on an optimally gratifying time of early mother–child symbiosis is very clarifying for the understanding of puerperal psychosis. At the time of age-adequate symbiotic closeness to its mother, the child is intrapsychically fused with her, not knowing who is who. Good mothering, saturating the child with libidinal, joyful experience, promotes in the child a good basic, though undifferentiated self, a resourceful foundation for its further maturation and zest for life. While the symbiotic mode of relating only slowly fades in both mother and child, Mahler and her team of co-workers observed how the child of 5 months, propelled by its unfolding, inherent potentialities, seemed to "hatch" from the mother–child common orbit, beginning at that point to individuate. While the optimal function of the mother during the early period of symbiosis is for herself to enjoy the bodily and emotional closeness to her child, she will from now on have to adjust to the growing independency needs of her child, while remaining an unfailing, stable support and home base for its excursions into the wide world.

During the first three years of its life the child has to accomplish a definite maturational task, implying characteristic subphases of a separation-individuation process (separation from the intrapsychic fusion with mother). This process is an integral part of the mother relationship, the quality of which has a decisive influence on the outcome of the process and on the child's future life. At the age of 3 years the average healthy child should have integrated the primary splits of its own psyche. The "good" and the "bad" mother images, inevitably created by the young child through its own reactions toward the real mother, should have become united into *one* whole mother representation, far more realistically perceived. This implies that the child's own self, initially equally split, due to its hate when frustrated and its love when gratified in the mother relationship, now becomes united into *one* whole, cohesive, ego, able to bear ambivalence without falling apart in splits. The real mother with whom the child was once united in symbiotic happiness will in one way be lost to the child as an extension of its own self. However, there has been an ongoing internalization of this symbiotic relationship, which in the end will become the child's internal possession. In real life symbiotic fusion is gradually replaced by an object relationship. This basic level of integration is, in Mahler's opinion, the prerequisite for securing the individual's later psychic health.

The process of separation-individuation is often a stormy one, throwing the child into states of ambivalence, rage reactions, and alternating dependency and independency needs. At one moment it wants its mother, at the next it rejects her. A good father means much to the child at the preoedipal period in its struggle to individuate from the early fusion with its mother.

Traumatizations of various kinds may interrupt the child's endeavor to integrate the primarily split self and to internalize the image of the good mother. Above all, the child is excessively vulnerable to separation traumas, exceeding its ability to hold on to the mother image in fantasy. The rupture of the libidinal tie to her at an early age means to the child a loss of the own libidinal self, as the mother relationship is still an integral part of its own ego. Too severe frustration of its basic needs for love and support may exceed its capacity for uniting the "good" and the "bad" into a tolerable whole self and a tolerable whole mother image. Mahler conceives of a spectrum of disturbances of psychotic and borderline character, dependent on the child's age when the arrest in its early emotional development occured. The internal structure of a bad-relationship will be set up – comprising a cruel, deceitful mother related to a part-self of rage, despair, guilt and inferiority feelings – "the bad self". The borderline adult personality remains with the profound ego splits stemming from these first three years, causing later maturation to be impaired by the "bad mother" – eventually invading actual object relationships – while the hatred and depression need elaborate defences to be kept under repression. Eventually the split ego is seen as an overt manifestation of chronic ambivalence.

Mahler interprets child psychosis as the outcome of a complete failure of the early symbiotic partnership of mother and child, in some cases probably rooted in an intrinsic factor in the child's mental make-up, in others due to the mothering person's incapability or ignorance of good early nursing; eventually both factors are operating. In the predominantly autistic syndrome (Kanner 1944) the child treats the mother as a non-living object, expecting nothing from her and refusing to communicate with the human world. Mahler views this state as the extreme, protective shell of a child who, for whatever reason, has never become enclosed in a symbiotic relationship with a mothering person. That this condition is a defence becomes obvious by the child's rage and panic when someone tries to break its isolation.

The predominantly symbiotic psychotic child (Mahler 1951, 1968) is unable to emerge from a grossly unsatisfying symbiotic stage or is thrown back into symbiotic fusion with its mother during the early process of differentiation. An extreme ambivalence has made it impossible for the child to create the image of the good mother, the only image that can be safely internalized. No inner core of trust and love is established, on the basis of which alone the child could have organized an ego and developed individuality. It remains fixed between separation anxiety and anxiety about intrusion, in a state of panic, rage, and ravenous object hunger, longing for the bliss of merging, defending itself against the threat of engulfment by the dangerous mother. It may also retreat from the frustrating object into secondary autism.

Mahler states that in this type of child psychosis the only adequate therapy is to release the child from its ambivalent fixation to the mother by making it possible for it to relive a "corrective symbiotic experience" through the intervention of a therapist. This will influence the disturbance favorably, inasmuch as the child becomes able to relate to and internalize a "good", that is a stable and supporting object, accepting the child in its own right. A therapy of the mother will eventually save her future relationship with the child. The prognosis is not too favorable, however; these early stages seem to require a time- and age-adequate meeting of the child's fundamental needs.

In Mahler's opinion there is a similar core of early disturbance in both adolescent and adult psychosis. We may add that this core is found in psychotic puerperal depression too, as a latent area of disturbance, compensated till it manifests itself at childbirth. Marion, in fact, also ended her treatment with a "corrective symbiotic experience" through her final restoration of the all-good mother of symbiosis. Marion's therapy has much in common with a child therapy, and we are able to discern the features of a belated process of differentiation, separation, and individuation. Though this process occurs here in an adult individual and is complicated by pathological development, it is, in principle, perhaps not too far removed from what goes on in the average child. One might suggest that the healthy 3-year-old too ends the struggle of separation-individuation with the final instalment of

the internalized all-good symbiotic relationship stripped of ambivalence, now having acquired a strong enough ego to be able to repress what has remained of the "bad" mother image – only to have a renewed battle for final autonomy with her in adolescence, analogous to Marion's experience in her second therapy.

Mahler found in the therapy of symbiotic psychotic children who had resorted to an autistic withdrawal from the intolerable object, that sadness and grief were the first signs that the child was emerging from its isolation and was moving toward the restoration of the libidinal object. This is also a typical feature of Marion's therapy. It is mourning that brings her lost, good, internal objects back to psychic life again. We are even able to catch sight of the core of autistic withdrawal, the subhuman figure behind its fence (drawings of 3 September 1965). From the moment the figure's hand breaks through the frame, Marion's mother appears for the first time as a whole person of intense psychic reality in the drawings, and Marion's grief reactions begin to unfold.

Marion's breakdown at childbirth was caused by an interplay of many unfortunate factors. However, a deficient early individuation seems plausible. The very core of puerperal psychosis points to an ultimate fixation at the symbiotic stage, though it may be discussed whether the later deterioration of Marion's mother relationship could have caused a regression to a state of undifferentiated symbiotic fusion with her mother. Here both factors have possibly been operating. Some early loss – a sudden, insensitive weaning? – could never be compensated while Marion's relationship with her mother continued to be fragmented and frustrating, never satisfying Marion's hunger for her love object. There was no "predictably reliable" mother there to interact with Marion through her separation-individuation stages; Marion remained with her split mother image, surviving, however, through her love relationship with her grandmother, which perhaps made her flight from her problems with her mother too easy. All subsequent rage and despair seem to have been canalized into the primitive image of the witch, constituting a core of disruptive power when it surfaced at childbirth. It is a thought-provoking fact that the grandmother, who had been a beloved substitute mother from Marion's very birth, was of peripheral importance – a fact reflected in the drawings – in comparison with the unsolved conflicts focusing on the object of primary libidinal attachment, which had prevented the basic integration of the own self. It confirms Mahler's statement that it is only through a real, growth-promoting interaction with this object that a satisfying separation-individuation can occur.

Marion's illness, illuminated by her drawings, has given us concrete evidence of the depth and malignance of early libidinal and emotional hunger, surfacing for the first time in the form of unbearable envy at the birth of her nine years younger sibling, whom she imagined to have gained possession of what she herself was missing: the all-good mother of symbiosis, of sensuous, close, warm togetherness. Her own deprivation again came to the fore when she herself was to be a mother. There was no libido to transfer to the child, who in turn became equally deprived and developed symptoms grave enough to require therapy before she was four years old. We catch sight of an illness pattern, transferred as a deep core of disturbance from mothers to daughters through generations.

During her last therapy in 1975–76 Marion became strong enough to cope directly with her all-good and her all-bad mother image without needing to keep them apart. Now she united them into *one* mother against whom she displayed her angry struggle for autonomy and independence. In its totality her therapy is seen to be a two-step process. During her first therapy the internal loss of the good object was the central issue and had to be remedied. Her all-important aim, requisite for her further maturation, was to get access to the good mother, reunite with her, and secure the internal possession of this mother with a lap and arms to hold her. During her second therapy eight years after the first one was finished, she struggles to get out of these arms, complaining that her mother is holding her too tightly. Marion's drawings of this situation may serve as an illustration of Mahler's description of a mother who doesn't adapt sensitively to the awakening independency needs of her child after the time of age-adequate symbiosis. The bad mother was as menacing as ever when she returned, reflecting the fact that this image had not yet been consciously elaborated and had retained its archaic character. Only a few weeks of psychotherapy transformed her, however, into a far more realistically perceived mother. As already described, such a "whole mother" representation with its good and bad features also means the achievement of a

coherent basic ego (at the age of about three), which is now able to feel and to accept ambivalence, having overcome its splitting into a hating and a loving part-ego. We may assume that this final level of integration constitutes the precondition for Marion's further maturation. This seems to be confirmed by her development in the last years following her second therapy.

In the severely disturbed patient the cry for reunion with the good mother is often a typical feature of the therapy; it may have different meanings in the dynamic sense, however, and the therapist's assistance has to be adjusted accordingly. Clinging to the mother image may mean pathological submission to a mother supporting only the dependent child in the patient who becomes fearful of growing up (see Masterson 1976). In other cases the longing for past security in mother's arms represents a mere flight from the actual tasks of life, or the avoidance of the struggle to achieve a more mature reconciliation with a realistically perceived mother. Often it means flight from the honest working through of the own hatred and rejection of the mother. In the frame of reference chosen here, these situations may all represent the conflicts "after symbiosis", and the therapist is right to help the patients free themselves gradually from the power of the mother image, thus overcoming their anxiety to face their conflicts. In an analogy Marion's second therapy to some extent serves as a representative of these conflicts, since the early mother of symbiosis is here securely preserved.

Through Marion's drawings however, the deep urge to recover the mother is seen in another perspective. Here is a psychotic core of early object loss. The recovery of "the good mother of symbiosis" represents the recovery of the basic self, and it is of fundamental necessity to struggle through the mourning and the rage reactions which have barred the access to this libidinal core of undifferentiated mother-child unity. This internal loss may be the "basic fault" of which Balint (1968) speaks and may explain his experience: after a time of benign therapeutic regression in relationship with a mothering therapist who becomes internalized, the patients begin to develop at a surprisingly rapid pace, this process amounting to a "new beginning". The same phenomenon is seen in Marion's therapy. After she has achieved access to the mother of symbiosis (the child at the bird's breast), the bad mother loses her destructive impact, and such a rapid change takes place that both Marion and her husband speak of a miracle, Marion explaining that she feels reborn.

As Balint himself states – and as most therapists know – this result is a rare one. Balint describes malignant regression in which the patient's craving, envy, hate, and misery seem to be endless. It may mean that no early love object is to be refound. In my own limited experience the course and the result of Marion's therapy have been approximated by a few patients, where a strong libidinal tie to the mother had been ruptured by a severe shock of early separation, which for various reasons could later be neither abreacted nor compensated. The intense affects connected with the experience of separation had been enclosed in an internalized bad-relationship which had remained unassimilated and split off till the therapy reactivated these archaic states through a period of regression. The core of the all-good, self-mother fusion in symbiosis had become inaccessible, and through this loss of the own basic self the patient's later sense of identity had been very insecure, eventually covered by rigid defences. The recovery in the therapy of this nuclear relationship implied the same profound agony of mourning the loss and the same working through of the murderous rage which once had barred the access to the good mother image. However, the strength of the latent capacity for love – in Marion above all preserved by her relationship to grandmother – made it possible to stand the ordeal of reintegrating what had been lost. These therapies have all been very dramatic due to the ego-weakness in this area of the self and have acquired the quality of a struggle for life, with severe crises on the way. Sometimes the therapist has to function as the new symbiotic partner to enable the patient to relive what is left of the real mother in her good aspect. Sometimes the therapist merges with the mother image. Marion remained oriented toward her own mother all the time, as the psychotic puerperal depression had brought her to the surface in all her terror.

17. The Therapeutic Process

"What we desire ... is that the ego ... shall dare to take the offensive in order to reconquer what has been lost" (Freud, S. *St. Ed.* XXIII, p. 178).

In January 1965 Marion had been in treatment for $2\frac{1}{2}$ years, including three stays in a psychiatric ward of in all 13 months' duration. Many of her conflicts had by now been elaborated, and she felt strong enough to consider ending her treatment. This level of stabilization may be the typical one for many patients with a psychotic core felt to be beyond integration.

Encouraged by me she had been engaged in drawing during November and December 1964. These drawings could not be seen as representing anything but an enjoyable activity.

There must have been an unconscious protest in her against such limited improvement. In February she again takes to drawing, this time on her own initiative. From now on she dives into deep waters, confronting a psychic reality of which she knows very little. Her drawings begin to reactivate her pre-oedipal or perverbal psychic structures, signifying that the pent-up affective experience of the very first years of life now becomes relived reality in all its untamed primitivity, though to a great extent experienced through the conscious trauma of the 9-year-old Marion, in all probability overlaying an earlier trauma of loss. From now on she is thrown into one severe crisis after the other. The repeated flaring up of affects and anxieties at a superficial level is directly observable to be due to a forward step in integration at a deeper level, indicating that a defensive position is being given up, releasing the bound emotional experience. Such a forward step in depth becomes visible through an unforeseen, sudden structural transformation of her drawings.

From the very first drawings onwards, her therapy can now be conceived of as a spontaneous regression during which she actively recreates in her pictures the internal constellations that three years before threw her into the state of psychotic puerperal depression. This regression, owing to a combination of fortunate and supporting factors, develops into a regression in the service of her ego from which Marion in the end emerges as a deeply changed individual. This process will first be discussed in the light of object relations theory, then from the viewpoint of the gradually occurring changes in the Id, the Ego, and the Superego conceptualized by Freud as constituting the three recognizable, functionally different areas of the mind. It proves to be all a matter of perspective and level of abstraction.

Object relations theory

What is here visible to every eye is that a new entity, a child core of the self arises, beginning a long development in relation to a malignant mother image. As indicated by Marion's own orange color, this part of the self obviously has the libidinal needs, it is actively stretching out for the lost mother, displaying its love hunger and frustration rage with an intensity unknown to the adult, compliant Marion. We meet with the internalized, "bad" mother and observe how intolerable she is, forcing Marion to concentrate all her affective energies in destroying her power, thereby replacing her own, former passive victimization by active self-expression and mastery. Through a series of internal events, constantly in the direction of integration and maturity, the child is finally reunited with its all-good mother of symbiosis, a restoration of the good object which is seen to constitute the very cure, revitalizing her whole personality.

Mahler's research suggests that the child's earliest experience of its own self is interwoven inextricably with its relationship to the mother images, at successive levels of integration, until the child at the age of about three has reached its first level of ego autonomy. We should accordingly expect the adult patient who regresses beyond the age of three years,

263

to come to terms with the more or less conscious mother images of earliest childhood embedded in the structure of the self. Recovery would mean to gain access to that level of internalized, primitive object relationship where the original failure had manifested itself; ideally, to resolve the pathological fixation and start the patient off with a "new beginning" (Balint 1968) or, as here, with a renewed attempt at differentiation from the symbiotic fusion with the internalized mother. Marion's spontaneous drawings reveal that this phase of her therapy really concerns the emergence of internalized relationships, archaic and distorted at first, between aspects of herself confronting aspects of her mother and her mother's representative, the hated rival sibling, at the same time activating the affects inherent in these relationships. Marion's emotionally colored conception of her "bad" mother had, without further psychic elaboration, been split off from the maturational processes and had therefore retained its fantastic, terrifying quality, constituting a core of deep psychotic disturbance. Facing and reliving these early bad relationships, the emotional energy bound up with these dynamic structures is liberated for the psychic growth process which we now can witness.

The very first relationship to be observed is that between the orange snail, the first representation of a "me" and the overwhelming bird, a "not-me" (drawing of 13 February 1965). The latter is an archaic, dehumanized mother representation, only symbolized by mother's bad colors, at the same time representing a condensation of Marion's symptoms, "hanging over her". From now on we can follow the differentiation of Marion's internalized self-object configurations, which change in step with, and in fact are organizing, the maturation of Marion's own ego. We observe how her development necessitates passing through the painful mourning processes, so essential for the reorganization of her inner world and for the restoration of her lost love objects and her own ability to love. In all, four phases of mourning are seen in this material, each with its own characteristics. Their comparison yields much information of why and how the dynamics of the mourning process differ, depending on the character of the relationship to the deceased and on the mourner's own relived maturational stage. The grandmother, the consistent good object of Marion's childhood, is regained early in the therapy,

probably making further therapy possible at all. Marion can experience her own hate and badness because deep down her loving and beloved grandmother accepts her just the way she is, good or bad.

However, the mourning related to her primary object, her mother, is the decisive one, depressive in nature rather early in this therapeutic process (September–October 1965) and turning into ambivalent mourning during the end phase of the therapy (September–October 1967). My experience since has given proof that the features of these two intervals of mourning are typical for the therapy of individuals who have suffered an early rupture in the libidinal bond to their mothers, causing profound withdrawal in the child and subsequently great damage to their further development. Marion's final, ambivalent mourning was very painful but did not cause too great problems. At this stage her ego had become strong enough to acknowledge and integrate her own hate and rejection of her mother, and to bear oscillation between extreme reactions of hate and love before a reconciliation slowly took place. This mourning process too – like the mourning of grandmother – ended with the "miracle", the instalment of the all-good object in internal reality. The very danger point, however, was the phase of depressive mourning, initiated by the externalization of the bad object.

Prior to this, the drawings reveal a tendency to circumscribe the core of the conflicts (drawing of 3 September 1965A), probably because Marion has now acquired the strength to do so. In this picture the internal world of good objects seems to expand, the split-off bad relationships seem to recede. Marion erects a fence around her bad self. I have suggested that this inner situation may be the typical one attained in a therapy of many borderline patients, with the supporting therapist belonging at this stage to the good, internalized objects. When stabilization tends to occur at this level, though still comprising a static splitting, it would in some cases probably be wise to let this inner situation be left undisturbed by the therapist's initiative; for the transition to the next level of integration is seen to imply a disturbance of psychotic dimensions, in other patients perhaps of far greater depth and malignance than in this case. Here the therapist's call for contact with Marion's withdrawn self (drawing of 3 September 1965B and C), causes an abrupt change in her transference reactions and her experience of outer reality. The repressed, internal situation is exteriorized (Fairbairn 1968) and overwhelms the weak ego, as the re-experience of abandonment – now by the all-bad therapist – becomes only too real. Marion has to go to hospital again for her fifth stay. A similar externalization of the inner situation had happened once before, just a few weeks after her drawing had begun to activate the powerful internalized object (drawings of February 1965), also then causing her prompt rehospitalization.

The conceptualization of therapeutic regression as an emergence of internalized relationships between primitive mother (or parent) images and equally primitive aspects of the self, is very useful in therapy. With this frame of reference seemingly inexplicable crises become understandable, because a very abrupt exteriorization of the bad object (the bad, internal situation) is typical of the borderline patient with a psychotic core. Better integrated patients externalize the bad object in tolerable doses. Both in my own subsequent cases and as a supervisor I have seen how this exterioration tends to disrupt the therapy. The patient may leave the therapy in a paranoid transference reaction convinced of the therapist's all-badness. Despair may cause an urge for suicide since life all of a sudden appears void of meaning. The unexpected experience of total isolation and worthlessness may cause a panicky acting out, the patient appearing far more disturbed than the therapist had believed. It may be the moment of psychotic disturbance in an otherwise non-psychotic patient. A change in the therapist from a neutral, interpreting attitude toward a more care-taking parental one may be of immediate relief to the patient, who to some extent will calm down, feeling sufficient support to enter upon the more or less pronounced phase of depressive mourning, a prerequisite for the subsequent abreaction of pent-up rage and revolt. Marion here seems to have illustrated the point of "catastrophic change" (Bion 1967) in the borderline patient, the necessary and inevitable moment of the growth process – providing the patient can stand it.

It is not difficult to observe how close Marion's own version of the treatment process is to the object relations theory of those present day psychoanalytical writers who use Mahler's research as the foundation for their own creative understanding of the psychic structure of the borderline patient (see Blanck 1974, Kernberg 1975, Masterson 1976). I will turn here to the very pioneer in the field of object relations theory, W. R. D. Fairbairn (1968) and without going into details I will point out some features of his theory. Marion's mother image has from the very first drawings onward a double aspect, reacted to as an intensely desired as well as a hated and feared object, approximating Fairbairn's internalized "exciting" and "rejecting" object. While Marion's "central" ego (Fairbairn), stripped of libidinal engagement, carries on the business of daily life without zest and joy, the developing orange girl in her initial drawings may well be conceived of as the repressed "libidinal ego" (Fairbairn), here emerging as a separate entity from the symbiotic fusion with the internalized mother. This libidinal part-ego, activated through the relationship with the care-taking therapist, soon changes from an observing (the orange girl) to an experiencing ego (the furious bird) and displays its drive-ridden craving for the lost, libidinal, "exciting" object. After the long struggle for mastery of the bad objects with which it constantly becomes confronted, the dependent, love-starved infant – the deepest split-off part of the libidinal ego – (Guntrip 1968) finally finds its place at mother's breast (drawing of 23 June 1966). However, when the libidinal object comes within reach, the dynamics of the splitting processes at once causes a mobilization of the "antilibidinal ego" or the "internal saboteur" (Fairbairn), which is seen in the same picture, violently resisting the further unfolding of this emerging libidinal relationship. This saboteur, comprising hate, fear, and stubbornness disappears when Marion accepts mourning (drawing of 22 April 1967). She seems to confirm Fairbairn's thesis that the libido is not primarily pleasure-seeking; its basic aim is the good object. It is this libidinal part-ego of love, sorrow, and rage, taking on various shapes in step with the level of integration and in accordance with the passions demanding expression, that in the drawings becomes integrated with the central ego. It is here depicted as the ego of general bodily vivacity and expressiveness, seemingly needing the hope of regaining the lost libidinal object in order to venture out of its hiding place again. The withdrawal in early life of this vital part of the self is observed to necessitate in therapy, a belated integration of body and mind or of body ego and the ego of adaptation. The pains of which Marion complained, migrating from one place to another all over her body, have also appeared in later therapies of deeply regressing patients, with or without the affecto-motor discharge reactions in the sessions. The patients themselves have commented on them as a "thawing", a "loosening up" of their own bodies; apparently some somatic process of change took place when the patients were again stretching out in the psyical sense from their state of withdrawal. They also felt some psychic pain or some impulse stirring at the aching place. Even the teeth were from time to time drawn into this process, the patients complaining of a transient, icing tooth-ache. Profound early withdrawal clearly has its bodily counterpart, the resolution of which has proved to be a lengthy process, also reflected in Marion's drawings by the subhuman figure gradually breaking through its frame (drawings of 1 October 1965 onwards).

It is in the patients who regress to the earliest years of life, that these internalized primitive relationships are most profitably taken notice of by the therapist. On another level of abstraction, however, and completing this perspective, the developing dynamics of this therapy may just as well be described through the changing relationship between the Id, the Ego, and the Superego.

The Id, the Superego, and the Ego

To the extent that Marion's drawings truly reflect inner states, we should be able to identify these entities in her drawings. I shall here try to trace them through her symbols and configurations to demonstrate that these abstract concepts can be understood in their immediate, clinical reality.

The Id represents in Freud's view the instinctive endowment of man, the libidinal and aggressive drives, as yet not filtered through, neutralized, and worked over by the Ego. It represents the vast, unconscious areas of the mind where the repressed past of the individual also sinks down, barred from motility and consciousness.

In the drawings the Id is represented by Marion's colors, the orange of libido and the black and red reflecting her aggressive urges. Her objects are given colors of their own: dark green and violet for the bad ones, yellow for the good, supporting ones. Id-impulses as unintegrated aggression are also projected into the outer world and into the image of her "bad mother" and are perceived as hostile persecution by the neighbors and by the witch-like mother. The furious bird, hanging over the sibling in frozen rage (drawings from 4 June 1965 onwards) may also be seen as an Id-aspect, representing rage

and desire exceeding at that time the Ego's capacity for integration. Though conscious to some extent, it is as yet excluded from direct expression. The same is true of the subhuman figure, seen to withdraw behind a fence into immovable isolation (drawing of 20 August 1965).

The Id is all the time depicted in non-human, condensed symbols, true to the Primary Process, that is, true to the primitive, image-forming way of thinking in the Id-area of the self where opposite feelings and ideas are intermingled with each other without clear categorization. These symbols tell us that Marion's Ego has not yet given the emerging conflicts access to its own realm of order and integration. Thus the subhuman figure (drawings of 3 September 1965) comprises the whole spectre of Marion's as yet repressed oral relationship with her mother — the depressive mourning, the frustration rage, and the pristine love, while its fence represents the inhibition — the fencing in — of their revival and open expression. At a later time a snake represents Marion's warded-off homosexuality (drawing of 27 April 1967 onwards). Only gradually are these Id-symbols replaced by portraits of Marion and her mother, that is, by conscious Ego-representations as far as Marion herself is concerned, now relating to an ever more realistically perceived mother.

The Superego originates from the earliest internalized objects, good and bad — that is, from the child's own version of its object relations with parents. Thus in Marion's case it comprises the earliest images of her mother and grandmother. We observe directly how they are "colored" by Id-impulses. Freud states: "For this Superego is as much a representative of the Id as of the external world. It came into being through the introjection into the Ego of the first objects of the Id's libidinal impulses — namely the two parents". (St. Ed. vol. XIX p. 167). Marion's mother image is at first unconscious, represented by symbols such as the bird. This image is merged with Id-representations — the bad colors — and projected into the outer world as something undifferentiated and threatening, destroying her life. In the small child early excessive rage reactions caused by too severe frustrations thus result in an archaic, sadistically cruel, core of the psychical organization of the Superego. The Superego itself is regarded as a formation of later elaborations and identifications, both with parents and with later loved and respected objects, though its final structure is largely determined by the outcome of the oedipal difficulties at the age of four to five years. For a long time Marion's superego representations can serve to illustrate another statement by Freud: "There is no doubt that, when the Superego was first instituted, in equipping that agency use was made of the piece of the child's aggressiveness towards his parents for which he was unable to effect a discharge outwards ... and for that reason the severity of the Superego need not simply correspond to the strictness of the upbringing". (St. Ed. vol. XXII p. 109). When a discharge outward of Marion's frustration rage is effected in her treatment, her internalized mother is seen to change slowly and to become tolerable, at last acquiring lovable aspects. Thus her internal mother's intolerable badness proved also to be a product of Marion's own primitive image-formation, nourished by her own, equally primitive aggression.

In Marion's drawings – at the level of therapeutic regression – we observe that Id-impulses of intense affective charge are directed toward, and all the time coupled to, primitive object images, constituting the dynamic structures of internalized archaic relationships. Freud, for example, in 1915 describes a phenomenon consonant with the later concept of internalized relationships. Discussing "a peculiar psychical inertia which opposes change and progress" he states that "... we discover that it is the manifestation of very early linkages – linkages which it is hard to resolve – between instincts and impressions and the objects involved in those impressions. These linkages have the effect of bringing the development of the instincts concerned to a standstill". (St. Ed. vol. XIV, p. 272).

It is these linkages – these primitive relationships – which in this therapy change through a series of mutations, moving from the state of unconscious undifferentiation towards ever higher levels of maturity. Even the most archaic object images – or, in this frame of reference, the most archaic Superego forerunners – are here observed to be subject to change when, through a period of regression, access is gained to the primitive self whose primitive affects create the primitive image. In contrast, Id-impulses will in more mature individuals come into conflict with better developed Ego- and Superego-formations causing conflicts of a neurotic structure, the working through of which is the concern of psychoanalysis proper.

Representations of more mature Superego functions gradually appear in the drawings. Thus

the guardians of the impulsive girl – her mother and her therapist – impose restraint upon her bad impulses, protect her from doing real harm and support her by holding her hands (drawings from 21 November 1965 onwards). In this phase she greatly needs her bad objects. Only in her last therapy of 1975–76 do we observe a more harmonious relationship between Marion's Ego and Superego. The protective shields of her mother and grandmother (drawings of 1 January and 16 January 1976) are felt by Marion as giving her security and guidance. She has now become identified with her grandmother's mild and loving aspects and with her mother's bold and courageous self-representation, using these qualities as ideals to live up to. Yet Marion's earlier conflicts with her mother have to some extent survived, inasmuch as her mother's protection is still partly felt as an impingement upon her internal freedom to move and as leaving her a space too narrow for individual life.

The Ego appears in the drawings as the various conscious "me"s. However, the very first self-representation, the orange snail, slips unawares into the pictures, being a still unconscious entity, merely identified as something good belonging to herself. Later Ego representations are conscious, they observe, act, move, remember, suffer, and develop. Through the struggle of facing and reliving the terrifying Id- and Superego-aspects of her own mind, Ego-integration is achieved. We observe how her Ego representations, appearing one by one in the various situations that have become conscious, are gradually pervaded by the red, the black and the orange colors, indicating their slowly developing ability to contain and tolerate ambivalent feelings without becoming fragmented into part-egos. At last they are gathered into one whole ego, "containing everything" (drawing of 16 May 1967).

In Freud's description the Ego controls the path to action in regard to the external world, it controls access to motility and to consciousness. We observe how the still unintegrated symbols are immobile – as if frozen – (the furious bird, the subhuman figure). Conscious experience is depicted as accompanied by movement – in the internal sense – as when Marion moves away from mother's house (e.g. drawing of 9 April 1965) or moves toward her grandmother (drawing of 7 May 1965). Her intense conscious affects are also accompanied by gross motor discharge in her sessions. The Ego is the synthetizing, integrating agency, capable of growth and learning. However: ". . . the Ego is identical with the Id and is merely a specially differentiated part of it – the Ego is an organization and the Id is not" (Freud). One can trace all through the drawings how Marion organizes her Ego at the expense of the symbolic Id representations, which in part are gradually thinned out (as the "not-me" structure of spring 1965), in part suddenly become transformed into a "me" through conscious re-experience of the repressed (as when the dissolving subhuman figure changes into the dangerous girl (drawing of 21 November 1965). Finally, the Id-representations disappear altogether from the drawings. There can be no doubt here that her pictures reflect the difference between psychic processes at the Id and at the Ego level. When the dreaded Superego-mother in the end loses her power, the treatment has succeeded in what Freud meant it to achieve: ". . . to strengthen the Ego, to make it more independent of the Superego, to widen its field of perception and enlarge its organization, so that it can appropriate fresh portions of the Id. Where Id was, Ego shall be". (St. Ed. vol. XXII, p. 80). Or in other words: Marion's pictures illustrate how the therapy, through gaining access to the psychotic core of her personality, draws both the Id, the Ego, and the Superego out of their state of regression, or out of their state of immaturity. The differentiation of the Id and the Ego is shown to have largely disappeared when she has finally achieved a better integrated personality, while the protective shields of her mother and her grandmother (drawings of 1 January and 16 January 1974) now correspond to the Superego of the average normal adult.

I have mentioned earlier the two turning points of her therapy which both caused her rehospitalization. The first is at the beginning of this process when the emerging orange core of the self confronts the overwhelming, archaic mother image. (February 1965). The second is at the moment of catastrophic externalization of the bad object (September 1965). From the time she got access to her mother's lap (July 1966) there is again a definite turning point of this therapy. After a few weeks' time she reports an improvement, felt to be miraculous. The impact of the archaic Superego structure has vanished and the psychotic core in herself is dissolved. Her former state of miserable inferiority feelings and chronic depression has now changed into an experiencing of herself as belonging to the human community in a self-evident, natural way, capable of joy and self-assertion.

In fact, after she has become able to feel contained in her mother's arms (drawings of 3 July 1966 onwards) – in spite of the "internal saboteur" – a maturational process is set going, comprising many different trends. Her arrested development, her standstill under the impact of the rejective mother image, is replaced by spontaneous growth, from now on felt to be promoted and supported by her mother. In the drawings an adult woman gradually replaces the child. At this deep psychic level the access to her primary libidinal object, the good mother, opens up for the access to and the maturation of her own sexuality. However, due to her still fragile Ego-integration, the menace from the primitive Superego is now replaced by the menace from the Id, that is, from her genital sexuality emerging from repression with an unintegrated greedy craving for erotic experience, threatening to disrupt her actual life situation. Through her general maturation these first crude manifestations of her sexuality become slowly integrated into a love relationship with her husband.

It is interesting that at this turning point she begins to report her dreams, while as long as the psychotic internal constellation had been predominant, she had none to tell except for a few, such as the dream of the witch that initiated her negative transference. This is in accordance with therapeutic experience: it is only when the psychotic episode is over, that dreamlife again becomes a feature of the therapy. Though one could hardly speak of open psychotic manifestations in Marion before this turning point, her drawings indicate that the bad object – the very psychotic structure – is only slowly yielding its power to her own developing autonomy.

The end of her struggle in the therapy of 1965–67 is rewarded with the achievement of the all-good symbiotic relationship (the golden picture of 28 September 1967) constituting an internal order of rather satisfying stability. Her safe anchorage within this symbiotic orbit makes an expansion beyond this orbit possible, her libido now being fully and freely transferred to her real objects of the outer world. At this time she has so much of a strong, cohesive ego that her final, defensive move to protect her good-relationships must be regarded as a neurotic mechanism of repression and displacement and not as ego-splitting, splitting being exemplified in the drawing of 27 August 1965 with a demarcation line between the good and the bad. However, again following Fairbairn, we observe that it is the image of "the bad object" that primarily becomes repressed, while the corresponding affects are displaced onto her mother-in-law, and that returns after the death of her father-in-law, again bringing Marion under the sway of the original bad object. The stability achieved in her first therapy proved to be only temporary, necessitating her second therapy to be consolidated.

The changing relationship with her external objects

As both her mother and her grandmother in reality were dead, there is no doubt that they represent "internalized objects". From her grandmother's first appearance in the drawings (drawing of 23 April 1965) till she is seen for the last time (drawing of 16 January 1976) her image never changes; she is the constant, good, whole object of Marion's life. In contrast, her mother image is fragmented and split, and the slow ascendancy of her good aspects over her bad ones is the core of the drama, occurring in step with the abreaction of Marion's rage. The unification of these two aspects of her mother in her therapy of 1975 constitutes her final level of psychic stability.

However, the drawings also reveal to what extent her actual, real objects of the outer world become colored by her internal object world, and how her relationship with them is subject to change in step with her internal changes. It has already been discussed how her own capacity for natural mothering is a function of her relationship with her own internalized mother image.

The conflict with the nine years younger sibling is concentrated upon the very core of all bitter sibling conflicts: I lost my mother to you. Marion and her half-sister had never competed at a more superficial level, about toys, favors or friends as siblings usually do, because as children they had never lived under the same roof. Marion reacted as a very small child to her half-sister being born, because her own early, unsatisfying relationship with her mother was reactivated, the sibling becoming the symbol of her loss. Had Marion's maturational level corresponded to that of a healthy 9-year-old child, her reactions would have been different. In the subculture in which she lived, the solution found by her mother was no rare one. The grandparents who had raised the child and functioned as its parents, often remained with the child when the solitary mother found herself a husband, a solution often found to be satisfying to all parties involved. Marion in fact has told us that she preferred staying with her beloved, kind grandmother than with her unpredictable mother. However, she had not at this time safely internalized a good relationship with her mother, and felt robbed by the newborn sister.

In the drawings the sibling appears initially covered by mother's bad violet and green, and is depicted as a huge monster with the power to destroy Marion's own world (drawing of 13 August 1965). Later the sibling is differentiated from the mother, appearing in her own green color as the hated, newborn sister to be destroyed by Marion — so far, a more realistic presentation of the truth (e.g. drawing of 11 February 1966). At last the sibling is thrown out of the picture (drawing of 30 March 1967), that is, from Marion's conflict area, while in outer reality Marion has become able to relate to her in a friendly, relaxed way.

The therapist, another actual object of this time, appears in two essential transference relationships. Initially Marion transfers her trust in grandmother onto the therapist who is seen in the good yellow color of Marion's supporters (drawing of 3 September 1965). During this phase the sustaining power of the therapeutic relationship is built up, so fundamental for containing the internalized bad-relationship that will later be exteriorized onto the therapist. The latter then appears as the violet double of the bad mother while Marion openly expresses her rage and revolt towards these two hated objects.

I have later learned to what extent Marion's internalized good grandmother modified the intensity of Marion's transference reactions as well as her hunger for the good object. In a few other cases too where an early traumatic rupture of the love bond to their mothers had occurred (in those cases well documented as severe separation traumas before the age of three), the clinging, the ravenous craving for the good object, the mourning and the destruction of the bad object have been far more intense and much more difficult to resolve. Although bearing the main features of this therapy, these other therapies had been far more lengthy. With no substitute mother and no surfacing psychosis in these cases, all the reactions which in the drawings here are seen as directed toward Marion's mother and grandmother were initially directed toward the therapist. In the drawings of some of these later patients, it was the therapist who appeared as the all-bad object to be raped and killed, as the all-good one to be loved and yearned for, as the "grandmother" of trust accepting the patient in her or his own right, and finally as the mother with a lap and arms to hold her mourning child who has come home.

The husband appears at intervals in Marion's drawings as does her fantasy father. She did not have the standard background with a mother and a father. However, as many girls grow up without a father figure, one will in this material have a chance to see how a girl comes to terms with her own sexual development without the classical oedipal triangular relationships. Her sexual development is a belated one, occurring in a therapy through regression to experience at childhood level, all the same yielding some information.

Thus it has become obvious that her capacity for libidinal love relationships is on the whole dependent upon the quality of the internalized symbiotic relationship with her mother, which is the matrix out of which all later libidinal relationships develop. However, Marion also depicts what use she makes of a father; she uses him so badly as a libidinal object next to her mother that she has to invent a father for the sake of her own development. This will better be seen through following the appearance of her husband in the drawings. In fact, stages of marital relationships are here observable at their various levels of maturation.

Initially the husband too, like the therapist, is colored by grandmother's good yellow color, Marion experiencing him as her protector. Depicted as a little clinging girl, she takes refuge both with her grandmother and her husband in a completely identical manner, overwhelmed by the menace emanating from the furious bird — that is, from her own, unintegrated, savage rage inherent in the split-off bad relationship (drawing of 25 June 1965 onwards). Marion at this time has no emotional investment in the sexual aspects of her husband, her self-portraits indicating that she seems to be too young a child for such interests.

When later in the therapy her revolt against the imprisonment of her marriage unfolds, the husband is not in the picture at all. What appears are the hated household utensils, the symbol of her feelings of dull slavery for others (e.g. drawing of 10 January 1966). Her drawings reveal that her factual

imprisonment is felt to be between her two bad objects of that time, her mother — and as a consequence of the transference reactions — her therapist, in whose firm grips Marion stands crying with rage and despair.

The father is the failing relationship of her early life, difficult to overcome. Her stepfather, coming into her life when she was nine years old, never appears in the drawings. It is the newborn sister who lies in bed beside mother (drawings from 1 October 1965 onward) betraying the early oral level of Marion's yearning at that time. There is no good father image to transfer to her husband, and he, like her fantasy father, remains without color, thus telling us that this is not a representation of an internalized, libidinal relationship. The only color her husband ever achieves is that of her good childhood object, the grandmother.

The first appearance of her fantasy father, acknowledged to represent aspects of her husband, is soon accompanied by important changes in her drawings (drawing of 2 June 1966). In this picture she raises one arm in protest against her mother's firm grip, stating that she needs a father to reduce the power of her mother. In real life her genital sexuality is now stirring, the fantasy father initiates the oedipal stage of development. He disappears again, to turn up three months later when Marion has gained access to the libidinal aspects of her mother (drawing of 23 September 1966). For a while he represents an idealized, all-good father with sexual aspects, Marion evidently trying to canalize her unfolding strong sexuality into a relationship with one, trusted, fatherly man, in order to counteract her own disruptive promiscuous impulses. She draws herself constantly as a child in relationship to this father who through his support liberates her from her exclusive dependence upon her mother. At this stage of her therapy Marion transcends her preoedipal fixation to her mother.

Then there is a sudden leap in the representation of male and female bodies. She and her husband appear as naked, adult sexual beings (drawings from 30 March 1967 onward), the lap-child going to disappear. Father and husband apparently have united in this male newcomer in her drawings as in some dreams of that time Marion doesn't know if she dreams of her "father" or of her husband. However, there is as yet no harmony between these partners. Owing to Marion's greedy erotic appetite she is torn by anxieties of losing her husband, both through her own infidelity and through his. Also her latent, homosexual trend is reactivated and projected onto her husband. The anxiety caused by her jealousy and by her own desire for wider sexual experience prevails.

Again there follows an interval where there is no place for a man. The mourning of her mother's death takes place. Marion is now able to become conscious of and integrate her homosexuality which is of a simple structure, merely a displacement of her libidinous longing for her mother's body (drawing of 28 September 1967). Shortly before, she had illustrated how she felt supported in her own genital heterosexual life by the strong heterosexual aspect of her mother (drawing of 7 September 1967).

Access to the all-good object of primary love (the golden mother of 28 September 1967) finally creates the adult Marion's full capacity for libidinal love relationships, both with her husband and her child. She now feels as her husband's equal in strength and worth, just as the long battle with her internal mother had made herself her mother's equal in strength and worth.

Marion, like an artist, has made something invisible visible. These pictures often come to my mind in situations with difficult borderline patients, as the drawings in a unique way illustrate the essential characteristics of ego-weakness. Marion seems to have grasped and depicted some basic configurations of a process that perhaps often takes place in depth, though largely unverbalized. Marion herself could not verbalize it; she could, however, make some comments upon her own drawings. Personally I see more and understand more after these drawings fell into my hand. They have acted for me as a "model" process, to some extent helping me in other borderline therapies to judge the level of stability attained, the points where the therapies tend to halt, the critical stages which have or have not to be relived, dependent upon the patient's resources. In many cases the integration that was attained in this particular therapy remains only a potential one. Not every borderline patient has had a substitute mother.

However, it is now up to the readers to make their own discoveries on the basis of these drawings.

Bibliography

BALINT, MICHAEL (1965). Primary Love and Psycho-analytic Technique. 2nd ed. London, Tavistock Publications. 307 pp.

BALINT, MICHAEL (1968). The Basic Fault. Therapeutic Aspects of Regression. London, Tavistock Publications. 205 pp.

BENEDEK, THERESE (1949). The psychosomatic implications of the primary unit: mother-child. *Am. J. Orthopsychiatry 19*, 642–654.

BENEDEK, THERESE (1959). Parenthood as a developmental phase. A contribution to the libido theory. *J. Am. Psychoanal. Assoc. 7*, 389–417.

BIBRING, GRETE L. (1959). Some considerations of the psychological processes in pregnancy. *Psychoanal. Study Child 14*, 113–121.

BIBRING, GRETE L., DWYER, THOMAS F., HUNTINGTON, DOROTHY S. and VALENSTEIN, ARTHUR F. (1961). A study of the psychological processes in pregnancy and of the earliest mother-child relationship. *Psychoanal. Study Child 16*, 9–72.

BION, W. R. (1967). Second Thoughts. London, Heinemann.

BLANCK, GERTRUDE and RUBIN (1974). Ego Psychology: Theory and Practice. New York, Columbia University Press. 395 pp.

BOWLBY, JOHN (1960). Grief and mourning in infancy and early childhood. *Psychoanal. Study Child 15*, 9–52.

BOWLBY, JOHN (1961a). Processes of mourning. *Int. J. Psychoanal. 42*, 317–340.

BOWLBY, JOHN (1961b). Childhood mourning and its implications for psychiatry. *Am. J. Psychiatry 118*, 481–498.

BOWLBY, JOHN (1963). Pathological mourning and childhood mourning. *J. Am. Psychoanal. Assoc. 11*, 500–541.

BOWLBY, J., ROBERTSON, J. and ROSENBLUTH, D. (1952). A two-year-old goes to hospital. *Psychoanal. Study Child 7*, 82–94.

BREEN, DANA (1975). The Birth of a First Child. London, Tavistock Publications. 262 pp.

BREW, M. F. and SEIDENBERGER, R. (1950). Psychotic reactions associated with pregnancy and childbirth. *J. Nerv. Ment. Dis. 111*, 408–423.

DOUGLAS, GWEN (1963). Puerperal depression and excessive compliance with the mother. *Br. J. Med. Psychol. 36*, 271–278.

FAIRBAIRN, W. R. D. (1943). The Repression and the Return of Bad Objects. Pp. 59–81 in: Psychoanalytic Studies of the Personality. London, Tavistock Publications, 1968. 312 pp.

FREUD, S. (1917). Mourning and Melancholia. *Standard Edition 14*, 237–258. London, Hogarth Press, 1957.

FREUD, S. (1933). New Introductory Lectures on Psychoanalysis. *Standard Edition 22*, 1–182. London, Hogarth Press, 1964.

FREUD, S. (1940). An Outline of Psychoanalysis. *Standard Edition 23*, 139–207. London, Hogarth Press, 1964.

GELEERD, E. R. (1956). Clinical contributions to the problem of the early mother-child relationship. *Psychoanal. Study Child 11*, 336–351.

GUNTRIP, HARRY (1961). Personality Structure and Human Interaction. London, Hogarth Press. 456 pp.

GUNTRIP, HARRY (1968). Schizoid Phenomena, Object Relations and the Self. London, Hogarth Press. 437 pp.

HEMPHILL, R. E. (1952). Incidence and nature of puerperal psychiatric illness. *Br. Med. J. 2*, 1232–1235.

KERNBERG, OTTO (1975). Borderline Conditions and Pathological Narcissism. New York, Jason Aronson. 361 pp.

KLEIN, MELANIE (1940). Mourning and its relation to manic-depressive states. Pp. 311–338 in: Contributions to Psycho-Analysis, 1921–1945. London, Hogarth Press, 1948. 416 pp.

KOHUT, HEINZ (1971). The Analysis of the Self. A Systematic Approach to the Psychoanalytic Treatment of Narcissistic Personality Disorders. New York, International Universities Press. 368 pp.

LOMAS, PETER (1959). The husband-wife relationship in cases of puerperal breakdown. *Br. J. Med. Psychol. 32*, 117–123.

LOMAS, PETER (1960). Dread of envy as an aetiological factor in puerperal breakdown. *Br. J. Med. Psychol. 33*, 105–112.

LOWENFELD, VIKTOR (1959). Creative and Mental Growth. 3rd ed. New York, Macmillan Company. 364 pp.

MAHLER, MARGARET S. (1968). On Human Symbiosis and the Vicissitudes of Individuation. Infantile Psychosis. New York, International Universities Press. 271 pp.

MAHLER, MARGARET S., PINE, FRED and BERGMAN, ANNI (1975). The Psychological Birth of the Human Infant. Symbiosis and Individuation. London, Hutchinson. 308 pp.

MARKHAM, SYLVIA (1961). A comparative evaluation of psychotic and nonpsychotic reactions to childbirth. *Am. J. Orthopsychiatry 31*, 565–578.

MASTERSON, JAMES F. (1976). Psychotherapy of the Borderline Adult. New York, Brunner/Mazel. 377 pp.

MASTERSON, JAMES F. and RINSLEY, DONALD B. (1975). The borderline syndrome: the role of the mother in the genesis and psychic structure of the borderline personality. *Int. J. Psychoanal. 56*, 163–177.

MEARES, AINSLIE (1958). The Door of Serenity. London, Faber & Faber. 119 pp.

MILNER, MARION (1969). The Hands of the Living God. New York, International Universities Press.

RHEINGOLD, J. C. (1964). The Fear of Being a Woman. New York, Grune & Stratton. 756 pp.

ROBERTSON, JAMES (1953). Some responses of young children to loss of maternal care. *Nursing Times 49*, 382–386.

SEGAL, HANNA (1973). Introduction to the Work of Melanie Klein. Rev. ed. London, Hogarth Press. 144 pp.

WINNICOTT, D. W. (1952). Psychoses and Child Care. Pp. 219–228 in: Through Paediatrics to Psychoanalysis. London, Hogarth Press, 1975. 350 pp.

WINNICOTT, D. W. (1956). Primary Maternal Preoccupation. Pp. 300–305 in: Through Paediatrics to Psychoanalysis. London, Hogarth Press, 1975. 350 pp.

WINNICOTT, D. W. (1971). Playing and Reality. London, Tavistock Publications. 169 pp.

ZILBORG, G. (1957). The clinical issues of postpartum psycho-pathological reactions. *Am. J. Obstet. Gynecol. 73*, 305–312.